Praise for the UK edition of

Accomodating Brocolli in the Cemetary

"Cook serves up a pleasantly diverting mishmash of word lists, puzzles, historical digressions and *Private Eye*–style howlers . . . as a browsable treat for self or others, it will fit that stocking-shaped gap in the gift market very neatly."

—Boyd Tonkin, *Independent*

"A serious study of orthography in the trendy form of a book of lists."

—*Times Literary Supplement*

"I started laughing as soon as I opened the book."

—Barry Cryer

"First-rate bedtime browsing . . . will surely find a place in many cultivated loos."

—Richard Jenkyns, *Prospect*

Accomodating Brocolli in the Cemetary

or why can't anybody spell?

VIVIAN COOK

A TOUCHSTONE BOOK

PUBLISHED BY SIMON & SCHUSTER

NEW YORK   LONDON   TORONTO   SYDNEY

TOUCHSTONE
Rockefeller Center
1230 Avenue of the Americas
New York, NY 10020

First Touchstone Edition 2005

Originally published in Great Britain in 2004 by Profile Books Ltd

Published by arrangement with Profile Books Ltd

TOUCHSTONE and colophon are registered trademarks of Simon & Schuster, Inc.

For information regarding special discounts for bulk purchases,
please contact Simon & Schuster Special Sales at 1-800-456-6798
or business@simonandschuster.com

Designed by Nicky Barneby

Manufactured in the United States of America

10 9 8 7 6 5 4 3 2 1

Library of Congress Cataloging-in-Publication Data
Cook, V. J. (Vivian James).
[Why can't anybody spell]
    Accomodating brocolli in the cemetary, or, Why can't anybody spell? /
Vivian Cook.—1st Touchstone ed.
        p.   cm.
    "A Touchstone book."
    1. English language—Orthography and spelling—Problems, exercises, etc.
I. Title.
PE1145.2.C65   2005
421'.52—dc22   2005041891

ISBN-13: 978-0-7432-9711-0

INTRODUCTION
Should We Worry About Spelling?

*   *   *

Many people argue that English spelling is terrible. George Bernard Shaw reckoned that the English "spell it so abominably that no man can teach himself what it sounds like." It is easy to find words like *their/there/they're* with the same sounds but different spellings. Some words have unique spellings all of their own, such as *colonel* and *yacht*. Fifteen-year-olds can't write ten lines without making at least one spelling mistake, and adults struggle with words such as *accommodate* and *broccoli* all their lives.

By contrast, Noam Chomsky, the greatest linguist of our time, claims the current spelling of English is "a near optimal system." He feels that spelling that departs from the pronunciation sometimes helps us to understand what we are reading. Silent letters like the "g" in *sign* connect one word to other words in which the letters are not silent, like *signature*; the fact that the past tense ending "-ed" is said in three different ways, "t" (*liked*), "d" (*played*), "id" (*waited*) but written only as "-ed," makes clear their common meaning.

The difference between Shaw and Chomsky comes down to how they think spelling works. One of its functions is indeed to show the sounds of words. The word *dog* links the letters to the sounds one by one—"d," "o" and "g." Italian and Finnish use such links virtually all the time. But in English the correspondence between letters and sounds is usually far less straightforward. Sometimes one letter corresponds to several sounds; the letter "a," for instance, has three different sounds in *brat*, *bravo* and *brave*. Sometimes two letters link to one sound—the "th" in *thin* or the "ng" in *wrong*. The sequence of letters can be out of step with the sequence of sounds; the "u" in *guess* shows the pronunciation of the letter "g," which occurs *before* it. Our problems with spelling are often due to not knowing the rules, say the doubling of "c" and "m" in *accommodation* or the consonants that go before particular vowels—*cemetery* ("c" is pronounced "s" before "e") versus *camel* ("c" is pronounced "k" before "a").

With some written symbols, you either know what they mean or you don't, say "$," "#" or "%." You can't use the spelling to work out how they are said. The second function of spelling is, then, to show what words mean. Common words like *the* and *of* connect directly to their meanings in our minds, rather than being converted into sounds letter by letter. Unique words have to be remembered as one-off spellings, such as *sapphire* or *chamois* (shammy leather). Some systems of writing, like Chinese, work primarily by linking whole symbols to meanings in this way. To use English spelling, you have not only to connect letters and sounds but also to remember a host of individual words, whether frequent ones like *an* or unusual ones like *supersede*. In other words, English uses spelling both for sounds, as assumed by Shaw, and for meaning, as believed by Chomsky.

English spelling is far more systematic than most people suspect. The best-known rule, "I before e except after c," applies to only eleven out of the 10,000 most common words of English—eight forms of *receive*, plus *ceiling*, *receipt* and *perceive*. Other less familiar rules work far better, for instance the rule that a surname with the same pronunciation as an ordinary word can take a double consonant, *Pitt* and *Carr* rather than *pit* and *car*, or have an extra "e," *Greene* and *Wilde* instead of *green* and *wild*.

The great asset of English has always been its flexibility. Starting with a stock of letters borrowed from the Romans, the Irish and German tribes, it has evolved with the English language for 1,500 years. In the Old English spoken by the Anglo-Saxons every letter corresponded to a sound in words such as *fæder* (father) and *riht* (right). After 1066 the system had to cope with a deluge of words derived from French and Latin, such as *tricherie* (treachery) and *nice*. Over the centuries it has adapted words from many other languages, including *coffee* from Arabic and Turkish, *broccoli* from Italian and *sushi* from Japanese. Whatever the language a word comes from, English spelling can handle it.

At the same time, the pronunciation of English has been

changing. Some Old English sounds died out: the "h" (pronounced like Scottish "loch") in *riht* became the silent "gh" in *right*. Long vowels changed their pronunciation between Chaucer and Shakespeare: *wine* was once said as *wean*, *stone* as *stan*. Punctuation marks were introduced and their use gradually stabilized, the apostrophe last and most eccentric of all. Because of the changing pronunciation, the rules linking letters and sounds became more complicated and the number of eccentric individual words people had to remember increased. The sound-based spelling of the past tense in *barkt*, *changd* and *parted* gave way to the uniform meaning-based spelling "ed" in *barked*, *changed* and *parted*.

All this change and outside influence has meant that English spelling now presents a rich set of possibilities for our use and entertainment. Pop musicians call themselves *The Beatles*, *Eminem* and *Sugababes*. Novelists hint at dialects, *ax* (ask) and *tole* (told), and think up unusual book titles—*Pet Semetary* (Stephen King). Owners invent names for drugs like *Zyrtec* and for racehorses like *Sale the Atlantic*.

It is indeed important for the international use of English that it is *not* too closely tied to speech. People from Houston, Glasgow, Hong Kong or Bristol understand each other's writing but might well not understand each other's speech. Much world business uses written English although the writers are not native speakers. Over three quarters of research papers in biology are written in English, and more than half of all Web pages. Spelling and punctuation seldom betray whether an English-language newspaper comes from Santiago, Kuala Lumpur or Jerusalem, apart from the choice between American and British styles of spelling in words like *labor/labour*.

So do we need to get excited about the mistakes that people make with spelling? Mistakes don't necessarily prevent our understanding the message. We still know what *extasy*, *Mens Toilets* or *england* mean. Spell checkers can now handle most of these mistakes without any trouble. A mistake that interferes with the meaning of the message is more serious. The writer may need help or the spelling system itself may need modifying. Yet we hardly notice similar problems in speech: people are not sent to speech therapy for mispronouncing odd words. No one suggests that *spoken* English should be reformed because some people find it hard to say "th" sounds. The most talented writers make spelling mistakes. Keats once spelled *fruit* as *furuit*, Walt Whitman wrote *depressed* as *deprest* and Hemingway wrote *professional* as *proffessional*. Does this detract in any way from their achievements?

Our discussions of spelling often suggest that there is an ideal of perfect spelling that people should strive for. Correct spelling and punctuation are seen as injunctions carved on tablets of stone: to break them is to transgress the tacit commandments for civilized behavior. Spelling and punctuation can become an emotional rather than rational area of dispute. No individual or institution has ever had the right to lay down the rules of English spelling. Nor are public discussions usually based on accounts of how modern spelling actually works, but on the traditional rules handed down from the grammarians of the eighteenth century. Attempts to meddle with the spelling without this kind of factual basis have often been disastrous in the past, landing us with the "b" of *debt* and the "c" of *scissors*.

The English writing system is the rich and fertile creation of those who use English. Its rules are the ongoing living response to how people express their ideas in writing in an ever-developing and changing world. Rather than continually carping about the decline of the English language, as people have been doing since at least the sixteenth century, we should try to understand and develop the amazing resource that is available to us.

This book, then, celebrates the richness and resourcefulness of English spelling, taking examples from real-life use. Its contents are not set out in any particular sequence. There are tests on various aspects of spelling with answers at the back. Also at the back is a thematic guide for those who want to follow particular themes such as novel spellings, spelling mistakes or the history of spelling.

THE ROUTE OF THE
ENGLISH ALPHABET

* * *

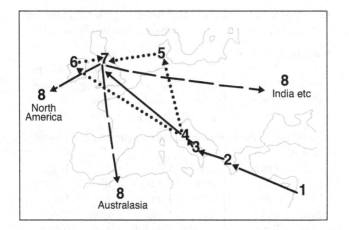

1. Phoenician (22 letters, no vowels),   𐤀 𐤁 𐤂 𐤃 𐤄 𐤅
    8th to 1st centuries B.C.
2. Early Greek (24), 8th century B.C.   Α Β Γ Δ Ε F
3. Etruscan (26), 6th century B.C.   𐌀 𐌁 𐌂 𐌃 𐌄 𐌅
4. Roman (26), A.D. 114   A B C D E F G
5. Germanic Runes (24),   ᚠ ᚢ ᚦ ᚩ ᛗ ᚠ ᚷ
    4th to 7th centuries A.D.
6. Irish (25), 7th century A.D.   a b c ꝺ e
7. Old English (*c.* 24), 10th century A.D.   a b c ꝺ e ꝼ ȝ
8. Modern English   a b c d e f g

The word *alphabet* itself comes from the Phoenician *aleph* 𐤀
(ox—rotate 90° to see the horns) and *beth* 𐤁 (house).

FLATTS AND SHARPES
Spelling Surnames

*   *   *

As well as starting with a capital letter, English surnames are often spelled differently from ordinary nouns or adjectives by:

- **adding a silent "e"**

bowls	Bowles	fry	Frye	trollop	Trollope
clerk	Clarke	green	Greene	young	Younge
coats	Coates	oaks	Oakes	wait	Waite
ford	Forde	penny	Penney	wild	Wilde

- **doubling the final consonant** (and sometimes adding an "e" as well)

angel	Angell	crib	Cribb	leg	Legge
bar	Barr	cuts	Cutts	lily	Lilley
bib	Bibb	done	Donne	lug	Lugg
bud	Budd	fag	Fagg	man	Mann
bun	Bunn	faithful	Faithfull	nun	Nunn
but	Butt	fat	Fatt	pot	Potts
car	Carr	fin	Finn	star	Starr
chapel	Chappell	flat	Flatt	tab	Tabb
club	Clubb	fur	Furr	war	Warr
cop	Copp	hog	Hogg	web	Webb
crab	Crabbe	kid	Kidd	wren	Wrenn

- **using "y" instead of "i"**

blithe	Blythe	miles	Myles	tie	Tye
crier	Cryer	pie	Pye	tiler	Tyler
kid	Kydd	smith	Smythe	wild	Wylde
kite	Kyte	tailor	Taylor	win	Wyn

Movie stars that fit the pattern

Randall Cobb	Leslie Mann	Brad Pitt
Johnny Depp	Demi Moore	Anthony Quinn
Sherilyn Fenn	Julie Parrish	Tim Robbins
Jack Lemmon	Sean Penn	Winona Ryder

GOURM KIT WITH HKPS:
Classified Real Estate Ads

* * *

Before you buy property from a classified ad you need a training course in the abbreviations in American newspapers.

Size

4br/den/2.5ba	2.5 ba 2 gr	2BR twnhme
1,800 sf	3bd	2,380 s.f.

Rms

bonus rms	Liv rm	mstr suite w/gas fp
formal din rm	weight rm	full warr. Bedrm

Kits

gourmet kitch	gourm kit	huge kit
new kitc	new kitch	

Gars

att gar	hkups	dbl gar
Carpt	RV prkng	

Special features

14 ft clgs frpl	Wood wraped	secluded PUD
Compl. updtd	windows	Excellent cond.
blt-in bkcases	Orig wd wk	Secure bld.
hrdwd flrs	appls stay	

Amenities

golf crse	PvtLndspdGrounds	lge wooded lot
pvt bch	IngrdPoolw/spa	cent. air
shy 3 Acres	great nghbrhd	big bkyd
24-hour drmn service	Prvt setting	perfect lndscp.

Prices

$900 dwn	30 yr fixed mt

DIFFICULT WORDS SPELLING TEST

* * *

Circle whichever one is right. Answers on page 151. Note in some cases *Webster's Unabridged* gives more than one possibility as a variant.

1.	dessicate	desiccate	desicate
2.	ecstasy	exstacy	ecstacy
3.	milenium	millenium	millennium
4.	dumbel	dumbbell	dumbell
5.	seperate	separate	seperete
6.	necesary	neccesary	necessary
7.	peddler	pedler	pedlar
8.	minuscule	miniscule	minniscule
9.	adress	adres	address
10.	accomodate	accommodate	acommodate
11.	iresistible	irresistable	irresistible
12.	liaison	liaision	liason
13.	harras	harrass	harass
14.	definitely	definately	difinately
15.	ocurence	occurrence	occurence
16.	embarass	embaras	embarrass
17.	pronounciation	pronounceation	pronunciation
18.	independant	independent	indipendent
19.	questionnaire	questionairre	questionaire
20.	wiered	weird	wierd
21.	brocolli	broccolli	broccoli
22.	refering	referring	refferring
23.	recommend	recomend	reccommend
24.	cemetery	semetary	cematary

NOAH WEBSTER
On Spelling (1828)

* * *

From the period of the first Saxon writings, our language has been suffering changes in orthography. The first writers, having no guide but the ear, followed each his own judgment or fancy; and hence a great portion of Saxon words are written with different letters, by different authors; most of them are written two or three different ways, and some of them, fifteen or twenty. To this day, the orthography of some classes of words is not entirely settled; and in others, it is settled in a manner to confound the learner and mislead him into a false pronunciation. Nothing can be more disreputable to the literary character of a nation, than the history of English orthography. . . .

In regard to the acquisition of our language by foreigners, the evil of our irregular orthography is extensive, beyond what is generally known or conceived. . . . the English language, clothed in a barbarous orthography, is never learned by a foreigner but from necessity; and the most copious language in Europe, embodying an uncommon mass of science and erudition, is thus very limited in its usefulness. . . .

As our language has been derived from many sources, and little or no systematic effort has been made to reduce the orthography to any regularity, the pronunciation of the language is subject to numerous anomalies. Each of our vowels has several different sounds; and some of the consonants represent very different articulations of the organs. That part of the language which we have received from the Latin, is easily subjected to a few general rules of pronunciation. The same is the fact with most of the derivatives from the Greek. Many words of French retain their French orthography, which leads to a very erroneous pronunciation in English; and a large portion of our monosyllabic words of Saxon origin are extremely irregular. . . .

THE SKIRT WITH THE SHIRT
Words with Two Faces

* * *

English often incorporated the same word from two languages with slightly different spellings. Sometimes the meanings differ so much that no one would notice their common source. Sometimes they still bear some resemblance of meaning.

Scandinavian
Words from the Viking settlements in England (about 850–1066 A.D.) came in alongside the Old English equivalent. Often the difference is between an English "sh" pronunciation and a Scandinavian "k":

> shirt/skirt, ditch/dyke, child/kid, bench/bank, shatter/scatter, shriek/screech

Anglo-Norman
The French spoken in England after the Norman Conquest (1066) came from Normandy rather than Paris. Hence English often has pairs of words from both sources, for example the Anglo-Norman "w" versus the Parisian "g":

> ward/guard, wage/gauge, warden/guardian, wile/guile,
> war/guerrilla (possibly Spanish), warranty/guarantee

Others:

> catch/chase, cattle/chattel

Which of these pairs originally from the same word do you still think of as having similar meanings?

differ/defer	canvas/canvass	whole/hale
metal/mettle	person/parson	of/off
plait/pleat	price/prize	broach/brooch
temper/tamper	calibre/caliper	plain/plane
course/coarse	discreet/discrete	flower/flour
artist/artiste	blond/blonde	draught/draft
feint/faint	human/humane	lightening/lightning
troop/troupe	arch/arc	

SPELLING AND MEANING

*   *   *

While most people see English spelling as connecting speech sounds with written letters, Noam and Carol Chomsky claim that it is a system for connecting symbols with meaning, rather like Chinese. It is the meaning that is shown directly in "$," "%," "&," "-ed" and "+," not the pronunciation. The advantages of this are:

- **silent letters show connections between words with related meanings in which the silent letter *is* pronounced**

"g"	sign/signature	"b"	bomb/bombard
"k"	know/acknowledge	"n"	autumn/autumnal
"t"	soften/soft	"c"	muscle/muscular
"d"	handkerchief/hand	"w"	two/twin

- **keeping spelling the same connects word families despite different pronunciations**

"c"	critic/criticize	"i"	decide/decision
"e"	extreme/extremity	"a"	nation/national/
"c"	medicate/medicine		nationalist
"a"	telegraph/telegraphic/	"o"	photograph/photographer
	telegraphy	"g"	sagacity/sage
"o"	one/only	"i"	child/children
"ea"	meaning/meant	"a"	image/imagine
"e"	college/collegiate	"s"	revise/revision

- **keeping word endings the same, despite different pronunciations, preserves the common meaning**

"ed" past tense	said "d":	opened, uttered, wagged, lodged . . .
	said "t":	liked, rushed, watched . . .
	said "id":	waited, parted, insisted . . .
"s" plural	said "s":	cups, units, packs . . .
	said "z":	miles, pounds, times . . .
	said "iz":	wages, matches . . .

- **some exceptions where spelling changes, not meaning:**

four/forty	high/height	jelly/gelid
fire/fiery	speak/speech	strategy/stratagem

LITTERARY SUSTINENCE
Poets' and Writers' Mistakes

*   *   *

These spelling mistakes (and some punctuation mistakes) by famous poets and writers are mostly taken from editions showing the original manuscripts of their writings.

Emily Dickinson
words: extasy, extatic, boquet, Febuary, nescessity, nescessary, unannointed, teazing, bretheren, independant, boddice, shily, witheld

apostrophes: does'nt, did'nt, it's solemn abbeys, it's dripping feet

Ezra Pound
words: tarrif, diarhoa, damd, supercedes, indespensible, sustinence, devines (verb), assylum, wierd, assininities

apostrophes: cant, dont, isnt, wouldnt, thats, wont

William Wordsworth
words: eughtrees, questined, craggs, vullgar, untill, lillies, pennyless, impressd, fellt, receved, anixious, plungd, th (the), whith (with), strage (strange)

apostrophes: your's

W. B. Yeats
words: proffesrship, origonol, descreetly, a complementary allusion, devided, immitation, peculearitys, beleive, sattelites, salid (salad), ceifly, seperate, litterary

apostrophes: 'till, Unwins reader, Mathers letter

Walt Whitman
words: staid (stayed), opprest, propt, almanack, deprest

apostrophes: dont, surpass'd, havn't

8

Virginia Woolf
words: pannelled, naiv
apostrophes: cant, shant, wont, dont, wouldnt, isnt, thats, your
  a woman of genius, I feel sure your worse, Prima Donna's, a
  childs highchair, a donkeys head, fathers state, the Fabians
  discourse

Ernest Hemingway
words: archiologist, condences, mirricle, proffessional, ungry,
  mistyque, useing, Hawaia, loseing
apostrophes: didnt, dont, couldnt, in ones life time

Many of these mistakes are essentially the same as those on
today's Web pages. Some may have been a spelling variant at
the time the person was writing or may, indeed, have been
deliberately chosen for various reasons. The four mistakes in
the first ten lines of "Ode to Autumn" compare with the 1.6
found on average in every ten lines of fifteen-year-old children's
essays.

John Keats

ODE TO AUTUMN *(manuscript)*

Season of Mists and mellow fruitfulness
Close bosom friend of the maturing sun
Conspiring with him how to load and bless
The Vines with fruit that round the thatch eves run
To bend with apples the moss'd cottage trees
And fill all furuits with sweeness to the core
To swell the gourd, and plump the hazle shells
With a white kernel; to set budding more
And still more later flowers for the bees
Until they think wam days with never cease
For Summer has o'erbrimm'd their clammy cells

THE THREE-LETTER RULE

*　*　*

Many short English words have the same pronunciation but different spellings.

oh	owe	an	Ann	we	wee
by	bye, buy	in	inn	be	bee
to	two, too	no	know	I	eye, aye
or	ore, oar, awe	so	sew, sow		

THE RULE

Words that are closely tied into the sentence, like "to" and "so"—called "structure" words—have fewer than three letters. Ordinary "content" words, like nouns and verbs, etc., can be any length from three letters upward ("bee" and "sew"), but must *not* have fewer than three letters:

One- or two-letter structure words	*More-than-two-letter content words*
They went *by* boat.	They went to *buy* a boat.
She flew *to* Paris.	They had *two* children.
Gold *or* brown dirt.	Gold *ore*, brown dirt.
Oh dear.	What do I *owe*?
No, yourself.	*Know* yourself.
I think *so*.	I think: *sew*.
We men must stand tall.	*Wee* men must stand tall.
Be safe.	*Bee*-safe.
I drop.	*eye*-drop.

EXCEPTIONS

content words with two letters: go, ax, ox, hi; spelling of musical notes (do, re, mi, etc.) (but compare doh ray fah soh lah), pi, id; letter names (a, b, c . . .); acronyms, AA, UN, etc.; printer's terms en, em.

Scrabble players' exceptions (unusual two-letter words): aa, ai, ba, bo, bu, jo, ka, ky, od, om, oo, qi, ri, xi, ut . . .

Some words have an "extra" letter to show they are content words: add, egg, ell, odd, ebb, err, ill, owe.

STAGES IN CHILDREN'S DEVELOPMENT OF SPELLING

*   *   *

1. **Prewriting.** Many children start by making marks that look like letters but do not form words.

   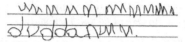

2. **Sound-based writing.** Children relate letters to sounds.
   - **letter names:** The names of the letters are useful in the early stages.
     soge soggy · *seds* seeds · *ran* rain · *bik* bike · *nit* night *bot* boat · *flu* flew · *tha* they · *He did in his sleep* died
   - **letters and sounds** (phonemes): Children try to make spelling fit the pronunciation of words.
     strabree yorgoat
     He dropted his samwisch
     she had a wobily tooth
     a little girl colde Lucy
   - **missing "n"s:** Children persistently leave out "n"s, perhaps because they do not "hear" them until they start to read.
     figz fingers   *lad* land   *feheg* fishing
   - **accents.** Children have problems in relating a non-standard accent to spelling "l," "th," etc. The following are from children who speak the Hoosier dialect of southern Indiana (source Treiman, 1993):
     pritty · *min* men · *thim* them · *fit* feet · *nels* nails · *keng* king · *rilee* really · *pen* pin · *beg* big

3. **Pattern-based writing:** Finally, children have to learn the patterns of English spelling that are *not* to do with the sounds of the word, such as:
   - **correct spelling of past tense "ed."** Children take some time to realize that the spelling of the past tense "ed" stays the same whether it is pronounced "t" as in "washed," "d," "played" or "id," "sorted." Even by eight years of age they are still getting this ending only 57 percent right.

FROM CWEN TO QUEEN
How Spelling Changed

* * *

The spelling of individual words has changed considerably over the past thousand years, as this sample shows. Dates come from citations in the *Oxford English Dictionary*.

magic	1386 magyk, 1390 magique, 1490 magyque, 1590 magicke, 1642 magick, 1776 magic
doubt	1225 dute, 1300 doute, 1483 dowte, 1559 doubt
yacht	1557 yeaghe, 1616 yaught, 1630 yaugh, 1645 yought, 1660 Jacht, 1666 yaucht, 1673 yacht
asparagus	1000 sparagi, 1558 asparagus, 1580 sparage, 1601 asparagi, 1711 sparrowgrass
island	888 iland, 900 ealond, 1275 illond, 1320 yland, 1546 islelandes, 1585 iland, 1598 island
hiccough	1580 hickop, 1581 hikup, 1621 hick-hop, 1626 hiccough, 1635 hecup, 1671 hiccup
subtle	1050 sotyle, 1400 sutill, 1422 sutil, 1566 subtle
queen	893 cwen, 1205 quene, 1290 quyene, 1400 qwhene, 1591 queene, 1622 queen
knight	893 cniht, 1250 knicht, kniȝt, 1369 knyght, 1400 knight, 1411 knythes
perfect	1290 parfit, 1387 parfiȝt, 1477 parfight, 1552 parfecte, 1580 perfect
cemetery	1387 cimitorium, 1460 cymytery, 1480 cimiteri, 1601 cemitory, 1644 cemetery
scissors	1384 sisoures, 1400 sisours, 1530 sycers, 1440 sysowe, 1568 scissoures, 1809 scissors
whale	893 hwæl, 1220 qual, 1330 whal, 1386 whale

REASONS FOR CHANGE
- French influence after the Norman Conquest: queen, island
- deliberate Latin-based spelling: subtle, perfect, doubt
- loss of sounds: "gh," knight; "h," whale
- odd ideas about words: sparrowgrass, shamefaced (<fast)

TYPES OF WRITING SYSTEMS

* * *

CHARACTER-BASED *(symbols link directly to the meaning)*

Chinese 中文   中国 (China) 一 (1) 二 (2) 三 (3)
                    星 期 一 (Monday)

MINOR ENGLISH USE & @ # ☺ + 1 % 27 = π $ ✔ ✗

SYLLABLE-BASED *(each symbol links to a whole syllable)*

Japanese kana   にほん (Japan) い ち (1) に (2) さ ん (3)
                 げつようび (Monday)

CONSONANT-BASED *(letters link to consonants only) (right to left)*

Arabic العربية   الجزائر (Algeria) ١ (1) ٢ (2) ٣ (3)
              يوم الاثنين (Monday)

Hebrew עברית   ישראל (Israel) א (1) ב (2) ג (3)
              יום שני (Monday)

MINOR ENGLISH USE: no 1 had n e brsl sprts (texts)

ALPHABET-BASED *(letters link to all sounds [phonemes], both consonants and vowels)*

Italian Italiano   Italia (Italy) uno (1) due (2) tre (3)
                  lunedì (Monday)

Greek Ελληνικά   Ελλάδα (Greece) ένα (1) δύο (2) τρία (3)
                 Δευτέρα (Monday

Finnish suomi   Suomi (Finland) yksi (1) kaksi (2) kolme (3)
                maanantai (Monday)

APPROXIMATE NUMBER OF USERS OF DIFFERENT TYPES OF WRITING SYSTEMS IN THE WORLD (MILLIONS)

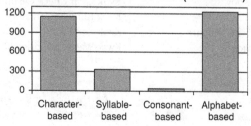

KRUSTY'S KUSTOM KOLORS
Spellings with "k"

* * *

At the beginning of a word, a "k" sound corresponds either to the letter "c" (before "o/a/u/r/l") or to the letter "k" (before "e/i") or to "q" (in words sounding "kw"). Many businesses have used "k" for "c" in product names, etc., since at least the 1920s, when Louise Pound said, "All in all, there is no mistaking the kall of "k" over our kountry, our kurious kontemporary kraving for it, and its konspicuous use in the klever koinages of kommerce."

Krazy businesses

Krazy Korner

Kid Krazy

Krazy Cool Kustomz

R-U-Krazy Inc.

Krazy Koyote Bar & Grill

Krazy Kapers

Krusty businesses

Krustys Power Wash

Krustee's Pizza

Golden Krust

Krusty's Bar

Tropical Krust

Krustys Bakery

Kar firms

Konsigned Kar Korner

Kar Krafters Inc.

Kut Rate Kar Rental

Klassy KARZ

Danca's Kar Korral Inc.

Kar Kolors

Kar Konnection

Kwality KARS

Kwick businesses

Kwick Kopy

Kar Kwik

Kwik Ticket Bellaire

PIK Kwick

Kwik Cash Check Cashing

Kwik Kill Exterminators

Kwik-Kopy Inc.

Kwik-Wash Laundries LP

Houston, Texas

Keyboard Kastle	Allie Kat Candles
Kay's Kurios	Aqua Kare Inc.
Culinary Kreations	Hartz Krispy Chicken
Gotcha Kovered	Breakfast Klub
Hair Korral	Kustom KutPG

TEST
American or British Style of Spelling?

*   *   *

		American	British	Both
1.	honour	☐	☐	☐
2.	meter	☐	☐	☐
3.	mediaeval	☐	☐	☐
4.	catalyze	☐	☐	☐
5.	labor	☐	☐	☐
6.	waggon	☐	☐	☐
7.	favour	☐	☐	☐
8.	neighbor	☐	☐	☐
9.	travelling	☐	☐	☐
10.	encyclopedia	☐	☐	☐
11.	moustache	☐	☐	☐
12.	color	☐	☐	☐
13.	paralyse	☐	☐	☐
14.	extol	☐	☐	☐
15.	center	☐	☐	☐
16.	dialogue	☐	☐	☐
17.	molt	☐	☐	☐
18.	analyse	☐	☐	☐
19.	plow	☐	☐	☐
20.	sulphur	☐	☐	☐
21.	vigour	☐	☐	☐
22.	skeptic	☐	☐	☐
23.	catalog	☐	☐	☐
24.	enrol	☐	☐	☐
25.	archaeologist	☐	☐	☐
26.	fulfil	☐	☐	☐
27.	glamour	☐	☐	☐
28.	theatre	☐	☐	☐
29.	saviour	☐	☐	☐
30.	distill	☐	☐	☐
31.	litre	☐	☐	☐

Answers on page 152.

POSSITIVE ENTHOUSIASM
Why Can't Students Learn to Spell?

* * *

College students still make mistakes with spelling. Typical problems are:
- not knowing when to double consonants: usefull, accomodate, refering, fueled, finnished
- confusing vowels: independant, relevent, compulsary
- confusing words with the same spelling: knew/new; or that sound similar: quite/quiet
- making unusual spellings regular: well-payed, senario

accomodate
acheive
affect ("effect")
ammount
appendicies
aproved
asses
  ("assess")
avocets
  ("advocates")
bare ("bear")
beginers
catagories
choosen
compulsary
concieve
confidantly
controlls
corect
correspondance
definately
dictionarys

discrepency
dissappear
eazily
effect ("affect")
elabourate
embarassing
enthousiasm
forsee
grater ("greater")
hinderance
illicit ("elicit")
independant
intergrated
intermidiate
knew ("new")
layed out
lerners
minites
occassion
occurance
percieved
possitive

principle
  ("principal")
profficiency
pronounciation
pyschology
questionaires
quite ("quiet")
refering
relevent
senario
sence ("sense")
seperate
sited ("cited")
their ("there")
to ("too")
tradditional
universitys
usefull
vocabularly
well-payed
where ("were")

OBJECTS USED AS LETTERS IN SHOP SIGNS

* * *

THE RITE NITE LITE
Spellings in "ite"

*   *   *

For some time a small group of words spelled with "ght" has had alternative novel spellings in "ite"—"nite," "rite" and "lite" and so on. These are used more in informal writing in notices, etc., than in books or newspapers. However, they are also found in the names of many businesses and organizations, sometimes suggesting cool modernity: "Nite Hawks," sometimes old-fashioned solid virtues: "Done-Rite." They seem to have been on the margins of spelling reform for many years. Isaac Asimov and Melville Dewey (Dewey Decimal System Classification) were both supporters of "nite."

Nite

Nite Hawks	Video Nite
Good Nite Inns	*Late Nite Catechism* (play)
Nite Iceboat Racing	*Boyz Nite Out* (disk)
Skule Nite	Nite Rider
Friday Nite Improvs	good nite irene (pop group)
Phantasy Nite Club	Karaoke Nite

Rite

ShopRite	ValuRite	Load Rite
Rite Spot Cafe	Flow-Rite	Maid-Rite
Kleen-Rite	Kut-Rite	Thermo-Rite
Sta-Rite	Pik Rite	Rite Rhythm
Done-Rite	Dun-Rite Kitchens	

Fite

Fite Club	food fite	Fitehouse
Fite Bite		

Combinations

Rite Aid Nite Time Cold Formula	All Nite Party Rite
Spell—Rite—Nite	Rite Lite Rounds
Lite-Rite Light Controller	No Bull Fite Nite
NITE-IZE LITE LOK	We Roll-Rite Through the Nite!

A JOB FOR JOB
Homographs

*   *   *

Words with the same spelling but different pronunciations and meanings are homographs. Some involve changing to a capital letter, for example "Polish/polish." Obviously, some may not be homographs in all accents of English.

bass (fish/instrument)
sow (pig/to sow seed)
tier (one who ties/level)
wind (air/turn around)
reading (to read/
    Massachusetts city)
furrier (more furry/fur shop)
degas (let gas out/French
    painter)
axes (tools/dimensions)
do (verb/musical note)
row (line/argue)
hare (animal/religion)
tear (liquid from eye/rip)
invalid (chronically sick/
    not valid)
dove (past of "dive"/bird)

job (occupation/biblical
    character)
pasty (pie/pale-faced)
does (carries out/female deer)
lead (go in front/metal)
minute (small/time unit)
putting (golf stroke/placing)
wound (injury/turned around)
polish (make shiny/from
    Poland)
sewer (person who
    sews/waste pipe)
buffet (food/push about)
sake (drink/for the sake of)
bow (bend/weapon)
mobile (movable/city)
moped (past of "mope"/vehicle)

Now try to read these sentences aloud without hesitating.

1. Playing the bass with a furrier sound, the furrier fancied eating a bass.
2. The pasty-faced man took a pasty from the buffet.
3. Putting on his jacket, he putted for the green.
4. Reading in Reading, mobile in Mobile, he drank a sake for the sake of old times.
5. Sewing in the sewer, the sewer tears tears from his eye.
6. The minute numbers made him number and number by the minute.
7. Job's job was as a jobbing gardener.

AMERICAN VIEWS OF SPELLING

*   *   *

"It is a damn poor mind that can think of only one way to spell a word." *Andrew Jackson, U.S. president*

"Nothing you can't spell will ever work." *Will Rogers*

"Correct spelling, indeed, is one of the arts that are far more esteemed by schoolma'ams than by practical men, neck-deep in the heat and agony of the world." *H. L. Mencken*

"Don't write naughty words on walls if you can't spell." *Tom Lehrer,"Be Prepared"*

"Take care that you never spell a word wrong. Always before you write a word, consider how it is spelled, and, if you do not remember, turn to a dictionary. It produces great praise to a lady to spell well." *Thomas Jefferson to his daughter*

"Many writers profess great exactness in punctuation, who never yet made a point." *George Prentice*

"Spelling counts. Spelling is not merely a tedious exercise in a fourth-grade classroom. Spelling is one of the outward and visible marks of a disciplined mind." *James J. Kilpatrick*

"You're not a star until they can spell your name in Karachi." *Humphrey Bogart*

"Add one little bit on the end. . . . Think of 'potatoe,' how's it spelled? You're right phonetically, but what else . . . ? There ya go . . . all right!" *Vice President Dan Quayle, correcting the spelling of "potato"*

"English orthography . . . is archaic, cumbrous and ineffective; its acquisition consumes much time and effort; failure to acquire it is easy of detection." *Thorstein Veblen*

"They spell it Vinci and pronounce it Vinchy; foreigners always spell better than they write." *Mark Twain*

"You teach a child to read, and he or her will be able to pass a literacy test." *George W. Bush*

KURUPT PLAYAZ
Pop Group Names

*   *   *

All of the following groups have been in the U.S. Top 40 (apart from the Be Sharps).

Ways of inventing names for pop groups

letter names for syllables (a device often found in children's spelling): Eminem, X-wife, Qfx, V-male, Pay As U Go, L8r

number names for words: 2 Sweet, 4clubbers, 2Pac, 6 Teens, 2gether

informal spoken form of "and" as " 'n' " (a frequent form in ordinary speech): Red 'n' White Machines, Paps 'n' Skar, Bald 'n Spikey

"k" for "c" (a traditional novel spelling in English, often found in business names, see p. 14): Outkast, Uniklubi, Kaskade, Kontakt, Uncle Kracker, Krossfade, Kurupt, Boomkat

"c" for "ck": Roc Project

"k" for "ch": K-os

"z" for "s" ("z" is an alternative for "s" in a limited number of English words but not for plural "s"): Jay-z, 4 Girlz, Air-headz, Az Yet Feturing Peter Cetera, Ralph Myerz, Rascalz, Sporty Thievz Featuring Mr.woods, Youngbloodz, Def Rhymz, Young Gunz, Outlawz, Beginerz

consonant doubling: G-spott, Gang Starr, Puddle of Mudd, Caramell, Dizzy Lizzard

"y" for "i": Zyx, Sylver, Sylk-e, Fyne, Kevin Lyttle, Silkk The

Shocker Featuring Mystikal, Tymes 4, Profyle, Prymary Col-
orz, Big Tymers, Cyn, Def Rhymz

"i" for "y" and vice versa: Kandi, Cyndi Lauper

puns or sound-alikes: Raymzter, Reelists

"a" for "ar"/"er"/"our" (apparently associated with "rebellious"
tough speech): Rhythmkillaz, Floorfilla, Twista, Platinum
Bound Playaz, Gorillaz

actual spelling "mistakes" (fairly rare, as this might suggest
ignorance): Poloroid

"lil' " for "little": Lil' Kim, Lil' J., Lil' Mo, Lil' Flip

"x" for "ex"/"cs"/"cks": Xploding Plastix, Rednex, Xscape,
X-ecutioners, Xtraordinary, Trance Jax

odd punctuation (using apostrophes, capitals, etc): @junkmail,
&g, S.h.e., 'n Sync, W-inds, Fu:el, D!-nation, Di-rect, B'z4

"da" for "the": Da Hool, Da Mob, Da Muttz

lack of word spaces: Wiseguys, Americathebeautiful,
Amillionsons, Goodshirt

"f"/"gh"/"ph": Ruff Endz, Phreeworld, Phixx, Phish

extra letters: Skandaali

others: Afro-dite, Absoluuttinen, Nollapiste, Hoobastank, Fab
For, Floetry, Dis L'heure, 2 Zouk, Plusch, Salt5, Tiktak, Tena-
cious D, Tatoo, Zed, UGK, Jemini, Eye Q, Ginuwine, Be
Sharps (the Simpsons)

Make Up Your Own Pop Group
Choose one word from each column; the second column is
optional.

He!!o!	2	Ph8
Phiting	'n	Koldz
Kreetchas	8	Karavan
Screemin'	of	Cheez
Hunnee	II	Kriminalz
Muthaz	Woz	Xit
Dirti	4	Peece
Ir8	R	Sistaz
Phantastik	LikZ	Kryin'
Medsyn	B	B-trayaz
&U	C	Krusade

FROM "HWY" TO "WHY"
Old English Spelling
* * *

Differences in spelling between Old English (circa 5th to 11th centuries A.D.) and modern English

- Old English "þ/ð"(thorn and eth) = modern "th," "þing" (thing)
- Old English "æ" often = modern "a," "wæter" (water)
- Old English "sc" = modern "sh," "scield" (shield)
- Old English "cg" = modern "dg," "ecg" (edge)
- Old English "h" sometimes = modern "gh," "miht" (might); sometimes lost, "hring" (ring)
- Old English "hw" often = modern "wh," "hwȳ" (why)
- Old English "c" often = modern "ch," "stenc" (stench), or "k," "folc" (folk), or "q," "cwēn" (queen)
- Old English "g" often = modern "y," "gēar" (year)
- Old English "f" often = modern "v," "heofone" (heaven)

Here are some words of Old English, as typically spelled before the Norman Conquest in 1066. Which words do they correspond to today?

1. æsc	13. gēar	25. niht	37. tōþ
2. bedd	14. hecge	26. ofen	38. þe
3. cīese	15. heofone	27. riht	39. þicce
4. cild	16. hlāford	28. sǣ	40. þing
5. circe	17. hors	29. sceaft	41. þrī
6. clǣne	18. hring	30. scēap	42. þurh
7. cwēn	19. hwæl	31. scield	43. tunge
8. dēofol	20. hwȳ	32. scilling	44. wæter
9. ecg	21. lēoht	33. scip	45. weg
10. fisc	22. miht	34. seofon	46. weorþ
11. flǣsc	23. mōnaþ	35. siextig	47. woruld
12. folc	24. nacod	36. stenc	48. wrītan

Answers on page 153.

DE DOCTAH'S AMBEETIONS
Accents of New York

*   *   *

Showing accents by adapting the spelling is less common in modern American novels than in British ones (see p. 116 for London). Here are some depictions of speech in New York, mostly showing ethnicity rather than a New York accent itself.

O. Henry, *The Four Million*, 1906

De agent what represents it pussented me with a dollar, sah, to distribute a few of his cards along with de doctah's. May I offer you one of de doctah's cards, sah?

Where, now, will ye be drivin' to? . . . 'Tis drivin' for pleasure she is. . . . I want to see four dollars before goin' any further on th' thrip.

If yer don't know de guy, and he's tryin' to do de Johnny act, say de word, and I'll call a cop in t'ree minutes. If yer does know him, and he's on de square, w'y I'll spiel yer de bunch of hot air he sent yer.

Jonathan Lethem, *The Fortress of Solitude*, 2003

I tole you. . . . Now we gotta fight. . . . Think Gus be gonna proteck you forever?

John Dos Passos, *Manhattan Transfer*, 1925

A man vat is ambeetious must take chances. Ambeetions is vat I came here from Frankfort mit at the age of tvelf years, und now that I haf son to vork for.

Oh I'm afwaid I was indiscweet to say that . . . I'm dweedfully indiscweet.

You kin juss come an git it. . . . Soivice at this toime o night. . . . If my husband was aloive he wouldn't have the noive.

OPINIONS ON AMERICAN VERSUS BRITISH STYLES OF SPELLING

* * *

"The differences between American and, say, British English spelling are quite modest." *Donald Cummings, 1988*

"England and America are two countries divided by a common language." *Attributed to George Bernard Shaw*

"Although American customs in spelling have never differed widely from British, such differences as have existed have nevertheless been treated as though they were matters of some moment, as though the Americans had really done something startling to spelling." *George Krapp, 1960*

"All that can be safely asserted of the contemporary conventions of standard Canadian English spelling, when there is a British/American choice, is that the norm is not yet to choose either indifferently for the same word in the same text." *T. Pratt, 1993*

The Australian Government Style Manual "arbitrates on many of the currently variable points of English spelling, generally adhering to what is often thought of as British rather than American practice." *P. Peters and A. Delbridge, 1989*

"In spelling as in vocabulary the tendency to innovation and playfulness is noticeably stronger in American than in British English." *Peter Strevens, 1972*

"A somewhat lengthy list of words that are spelled differently in the United States and Britain can be generated from published discussions on this topic. . . . What is most noticeable about this list is not its length but its shortness relative to the full vocabulary of the English language." *Richard Venezky, 1999*

OPEN 8:30 TIL 11:00
Uses of "Till," " 'Til," "Til" and "Until"

* * *

"Till" was a separate word from "until" throughout the history of English and was mostly spelled "till" since 1200 A.D. Sometimes it is treated as an abbreviation for "until" and so spelled with an apostrophe, " 'til," and/or a single "l" "til." *Webster's* gives "til" as a variant.

Frequency of Forms of "Till" in Google

	Google
Until	93.0%
Untill	0.6%
Till	3.8%
Til/'til	3.7%
Number of examples	57,730,000

It is almost impossible to eliminate the Scandinavian word "til" from the Google scores, hence overestimating it considerably. Similarly, the British noun "shop till" distorts the figures for "till."

HY·PHEN·AT·ION
Hyphens for Line Breaks

*   *   *

One of the decisions in printed text is how to divide words that are too long with hyphens.

 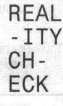 

Eccentric Hyphens

mans-laughter	male-volence	rear-ranged
fin-ding	pos-twar	ever-yone
unself-conscious	fru-ity	da-ily
rein-stall	berib-boned	se-arched
ch-anges	spi-noff	bre-akfast
the-rapist	pain-staking	af-ternoon

| RULES FOR HYPHENATION

British style tends to divide words up into meaningful parts; American style tends to divide words up into syllables. However, dictionaries vary considerably, many British ones using "American style."

American	British	American	British
struc-ture	struct-ure	mys-tery	myst-ery
trium-phant	triumph-ant	rec-tangle	rect-angle
knowl-edge	know-ledge	impor-tant	import-ant
geog-raphy	geo-graphy	infor-mation	inform-ation
inspira-tion	inspir-ation	commu-nity	commun-ity
desensi-tize	desens-itise		

Some syllable divisions in American business names
Bayou Ka-Nex-Shun Home Cooking
Ar'Ke-Tek-Cher Inc.

Awkward Divisions

MAN SHOT IN TIT

FOR TAT KILLING

Irish Newspaper headline

DISCRETE HANDYCAP FACILITIES
Foreign Hotels

*   *   *

While these come from hotels in Italy, Greece and Spain, similar facilities are doubtless available in other countries.

Your Hotel

nize, cozy and elegant three stars hotel · Would you like a discrete, warm and friendly welcome? · handycap facilities · fantasically placed for access to all the major attractions · modern and confortable hotel renued in 2001 · very clen and comfortable · All ages wellcome · spectacular panoramic views over the three famous golf course's · Italian garden with statues and secolar trees · important lobby in the low plant · nise environment · a managment that loves the ways of an ancient tradition of ospitality · Smiles and kidness are waiting for you · it rappresents an experience born to estabilish a direct contact between guests and the hotels · Emersed in Nature · Prices qouted are per night · Confortable rooms toghether with its renowned cuisine make the hotel an ideal residence in a unique place · Familiar cooking · Our fine cuisine, wich uses products from the region, toghether with our attentive service, meets the exacting standardts of our guests · a reserved and particular house, located directly on his own sandy beach · on leaving we'll refound you the cost of the 1 day ticket

Your Room

shared bathroom, for baoys or girls · insonorized windows · rooms With matrimonial beds · Closed captioned tv · hydromassage tube in suites · wasin in rooms · with luxury en-suits bathrooms · Bathtub At Bathroom · The accomodation has all the comforts and high quality implants · furnished with antique mobiles · Recently painted a-fresh by the owner · Brite new · In exclnt cond · Hi ceils · Children's' Bed Available · All Rooms Have Central Air · and a lot of beautiful things as accesorys · Littered with details · Thelephone · Tv-colors · The mini bar is adeguately substituted

Some of the Facilities
espectacular garden · landcaped lawns · bay sitting · Lit grass tennis court · Peddle-boats, canoes, houseboats · snorking · Escursions · 18 holes golf gruond, riding school, clay pingeon shooting · Bycicles at your disposal from the Hotel for your pleasur · the quiteness you need · indipendent entrance · adjacent to the principle structure · In the immediate nearby guests can find tennis courts · Start the day in a positive mood with our sel service buffet · Make a gift with venetian artesany · Campings, Bed and breakfast, Rent Houses, Hostels · busparking places

The Whole Package
In the next pages you will find three localities, where for only characteristics in their kind, for confort, tranquillity and landscaped harmony, they are between beautifulst of Italy. You will find apartments in rent, furnishes to you with taste, complete of every type of confort, every the most exasperated requirement, can be satisfied. The property puts highly to disposition of local referenziate persons qualitati to you, where a vacation is one mrs vacation and the satisfaction staff is better the provisions for a journey for one optimal working resumption. We wait for you for a visit without engagement, in order to show the fabulous places to you and the apartments that we propose to you YOU RESERVE YOURSELVES ENDURED HERE

An indespensable leg of a journey for those who want to know the "Magna Grecia," a necessary stop off for pilgrims of eastern spirit, a votive place dear to phylosophers who went looking for knowledge even within the volcanos. Agrigento was a meeting point for all the civilizations that have influenced the scene both externally and internally of Sicily and its proud inhabitans.

LIL' SPYDER
American Show Dogs

*   *   *

These dogs have all competed in recent U.S. dog shows.

lack of word spaces
    Mistymoor, Gonewiththewind, ShengCheeRightOnTarget,
    Meadowsbrookspatrioticbanner

letter and number names
    Y Not Simon, C. Clearly, Xtreme Hero, For-U-To-N-V,
    IT HAD 2 BE YOU, Bells R Ringing, B MY VALENTINE

"'n" for "and"
    Cheese-N-Crackers, Step N'Style, Up N'Adam, Lucy N Sky
    Diamonds, Up-N' Atem, Buttons 'N Bows, Top Hat N'Tails

"n" for "ing"
    Dancin Desparado, Hunka Burnin' Love, Gettin' Jiggy with it,
    I'm Just Chillin', Travelin' Man, Sumthin To Talkabout, Dig
    N' The Dream

conventional "novel" forms
    Hi Caliber Bullet, Mr. Saturday Nite, Brite Bernice,
    Nite Autumn, Hi Sierra, Sno Storm, Midnite Magic

"lil'"
    Rockin' Lil' Rascal, Lil Sassy Kassy

various puns
    Turn the Paige, Oh Oh Seven, Son Also Rises, Knot-A-Yacht,
    Bear Necessities, Steel the Show, Love Bytes, Boy Named
    Sioux, Blow Ye Aweigh, Speckle & Hyde, Look's Like Reign

others
    Bumble Brie Blue, Whimsical Winafred, One Formy Master,
    Ice Krusher, One Tuff Cookie, Megnificent, The Wiz Kid,
    Chicklett, Time To Rocon Roll, Mys Tory, Razaldasal Dolli,
    Xelena, Khlassic Hicliff, Kwontum Leap, Bar Nun,
    Khan-Frontation, Lotsa Spots, Shakn Not Stirrd, Spyder

SILENT LETTERS

* * *

Silent letters may indicate: different words: "whole/hole," "plum/plumb"; "long" vowels: "rid/ride," or "hard" consonants: "guest/gesture"; different forms of the same word: "resign/ resignation." In English, only "j," "o" ("colonel"?), "v" and "y" cannot be silent.

A artistically, dramatically, stoically, musically, romantically · **B** climb, numb, comb, thumb, crumb, debt, doubt, subtle · **C** acquit, czar, indict, Conne̲cticut, muscle, scissors, Tucson · **D** grandson, handkerchief, sandwich, handsome, Wednesday · **E** rite, fame, enclose, bridge, careful, cemet̲ery, hope, corpse · **F** halfpenny · **G** though, light, reign, champagne, diaphragm, high, gnaw · **H** hour, hurra̲h, khaki, Gandhi, heir, exhaust, Thames, ghost · **I** business · **K** know, knot, knife, knickers, knell, knight, blackguard, knock · **L** salmon, psalm, almond, calf, folk, yolk, calm, talk, Lincoln · **M** mnemonic · **N** autumn, solemn, damn, hymn, monsieur, column, chimney · **P** corps, pneumonia, pseudo, ptomaine, receipt, Tho̲mpson · **R** myrrh, diarrhoea, February · **S** island, viscount, Illinois, aisle, debris, bourgeois, fracas · **T** ballet, Christmas, gourmet, rap- port, asthma, listen, castle · **U** guest, guitar, catalogue, tongue, dialogue · **W** sword, whore, answer, Norwich, two, wrist · **X** faux pas, Sioux · **Z** rendezvous, laissez-faire, chez

CAUSES OF "SILENT" LETTERS

historical change: the sound has dropped out over time but the spelling has not changed: light, hope, knot · *addition of letters:* the letter was added to make the spelling more like French or Latin: debt, victual, island · *difficult sound combinations:* hand- kerchief, sandwich · *word borrowing:* the word was originally taken from another language: champagne, khaki, myrrh

SPELLING GAMES
Set 1

*   *   *

Hangman

1. One player thinks of a word and writes it as a series of dashes instead of letters, for example: __ __ __ __
2. The other player(s) have to guess what the word is by suggesting letters—"Does it have any 'c's?"
3. If the guess is correct, the first player substitutes the letter for the appropriate dashes. __ __ c __
4. If the guess is wrong, the first player adds one element of the hangman drawing, starting with the pole.
5. The game finishes either when the word is complete or the hangman drawing is finished and all the other players have been hanged.
   For the squeamish, the drawing can be the Stop Sign, completed in eight steps.

Guggenheim

1. Players choose (a) a set of five different categories, say, places, first names, vegetables, cars and sports, and (b) a word five or six letters long, say, "praise."
2. Each player has to provide a word for each category starting with each letter of the target word, i.e.:

	P	R	A	I	S	E
place	Poland	Rio	Aden	Ireland	Santiago	Essex
first-name	Paula	Rita	Arthur	Ian	Sam	Edith
vegetable	potato	radish	avocado	—	spinach	—
car	Porsche	Renault	Alfa Romeo	—	Saab	E-type
sport	polo	riding	archery	—	swimming	—

3. Scoring is either 1 point for each word supplied or 1 point for each word no one else supplies, each blank counting 1 minus point.

GEORGE BERNARD SHAW
Preface to R. A. Wilson, The Miraculous Birth of Language, *1941 (extracts)*

* * *

Professor Wilson has shewn that it was as a reading and writing animal that Man achieved his human eminence above those who are called beasts. Well, it is I and my like who have to do the writing. I have done it professionally for the last sixty years as well as it can be done with a hopelessly inadequate alphabet devised centuries before the English language existed to record another and very different language. Even this alphabet is reduced to absurdity by a foolish orthography based on the notion that the business of spelling is to represent the origin and history of a word instead of its sound and meaning. Thus an intelligent child who is bidden to spell *debt*, and very properly spells it d-e-t, is caned for not spelling it with a b because Julius Caesar spelt the Latin word for it with a b. . . .

. . . the waste does not come home to the layman. For example, take the two words *tough* and *cough*. He may not have to write them for years, if at all. Anyhow he now has *tough* and *cough* so thoroughly fixed in his head and everybody else's that he would be set down as illiterate if he wrote *tuf* and *cof*; consequently a reform would mean for him simply a lot of trouble not worth taking. Consequently the layman, always in a huge majority, will fight spelling reform tooth and nail. As he cannot be convinced, his opposition must be steam-rollered by the overworked writers and printers who feel the urgency of the reform.

Though I am an author, I also am left cold by *tough* and *cough*; for I, too, seldom write them. But take the words *though* and *should* and *enough*: containing eighteen letters. Heaven knows how many hundred thousand times I have had to write these constantly recurring words. With a new English alphabet replacing the old Semitic one with its added Latin vowels I should be able to spell t-h-o-u-g-h with two letters, s-h-o-u-l-d with three, and e-n-o-u-g-h with four: nine letters instead of eighteen: a saving of a hundred per cent of my time and my typist's time and the printer's time, to say nothing of the saving in paper and wear and tear of machinery. . . .

I could fill pages with instances; but my present point is not to make lists of anomalies, but to show that (a) the English language cannot be spelt with five Latin vowels, and (b) that though the vowels used by English people are as various as their faces yet they understand one another's speech well enough for all practical purposes, just as whilst Smith's face differs from Jones's so much that the one could not possibly be mistaken for the other yet they are so alike that they are instantly recognizable as man and man, not as cat and dog. In the same way it is found that though the number of different vowel sounds we utter is practically infinite yet a vowel alphabet of eighteen letters can indicate a speech sufficiently unisonal to be understood generally, and to preserve the language from the continual change which goes on at present because the written word teaches nothing as to the pronunciation, and frequently belies it. . . .

My concern here, however, is not with pronunciation but with the saving of time wasted. We try to extend our alphabet by writing two letters instead of one; but we make a mess of this device. With reckless inconsistency we write *sweat* and *sweet*, and then write *whet* and *wheat*, just the contrary. Consistency is not always a virtue; but spelling becomes a will-o'-the wisp without it. . . .

If the introduction of an English alphabet for the English language costs a civil war, or even, as the introduction of summer time did, a world war, I shall not grudge it. The waste of war is negligible in comparison to the daily waste of trying to communicate with one another in English through an alphabet with sixteen letters missing. That must be remedied, come what may.

A THORO PROGRAM
Did U.S. Spelling Change Work?
* * *

In 1898 the National Education Association (NEA) listed twelve words whose spelling should be reformed. Have they succeeded more than a hundred years later?

Percentage of NEA Spellings on the Web
This includes sites with British spelling, which seldom use these spellings (apart from "program" in the computer sense). It also fails to show the common use of these spellings in informal street notices, etc.

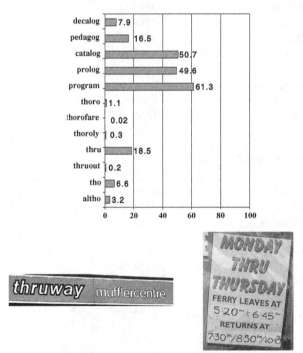

FNOMNL 4EN JUNK
American License Plates

*   *   *

Unusual spelling is often used to personalize car license plates.

Numbers for Letters or Words

CYNICL1	1NTSTND
SEEUL8ER	22 NICE
EZ4ME	2BENVD
2HOT4U	4EN JUNK
PD4BYEX	4GETIT
O2BINLA	2FAST4U
10SPRO	CD8D
1BUG2C	W84ME
81TCH	

Leaving Out Letters

HIP CHC	CHZHED
FNOMNL	QUIKNSS
XPIRED	WNDW95

Letters for Words or Syllables

XTAZ	IFLUBYU
CRZY 4U	ETBLVR
O2BNLA	1BLU BYU
9WONWON	CYCOPTH

Others

YA HOO	YESLORD
88 KEYS (Liberace)	

K'YARDS AND SICH THINGS
Southern Accents

* * *

In *Huckleberry Finn*, Mark Twain claims to use "the Missouri negro dialect; the extremest form of the backwoods Southwestern dialect; the ordinary 'Pike County' dialect; and four modified varieties of this last." Which of these four groups do you think the following characters belong to?

Jim: I didn' know dey was so many un um. I hain't hearn 'bout none un um, skasely, but ole King Sollermun, onless you counts dem kings dat's in a pack er k'yards. How much do a king git?

Huck Finn's Pap: I says look at my hat—if you call it a hat—but the lid raises up and the rest of it goes down till it's below my chin, and then it ain't rightly a hat at all, but more like my head was shoved up through a jint o' stove-pipe.

Jake Packard: What I say is this: it ain't good sense to go court'n around after a halter if you can git at what you're up to in some way that's jist as good and at the same time don't bring you into no resks. Ain't that so?

Old man: I've done considerble in the doctoring way in my time. Layin' on o' hands is my best holt—for cancer and paralysis, and sich things; and I k'n tell a fortune pretty good when I've got somebody along to find out the facts for me.

Tom Sawyer: I hain't ever done you no harm. You know that. So, then, what you want to come back and ha'nt ME for?

Mrs. Hotchkiss: You all hearn me: he's crazy, s'I; everything shows it, s'I. Look at that-air grindstone, s'I; want to tell me't any cretur 't's in his right mind 's a goin' to scrabble all them crazy things onto a grindstone, s'I?

Nowadays it is felt that the more accurately such spelling reflects an accent, the more it biases the reader towards thinking the character illiterate and uneducated. In Jonathan Lethem's portrait of Brooklyn, *The Fortress of Solitude*, for example, about the only examples of accent spelling seem to be "ax" for "ask," "tole" for "told" and "proteck" for "protect."

GENES FOR JEANS
English Homophones

*   *   *

As several speech sounds can correspond to each letter in English, many words have the same pronunciation but different spelling (homophones), the source of many puns and rhymes. Of course many homophones depend on the word being said with a particular accent.

allowed/aloud
banned/band
beer/bier
boarder/border
boos/booze
brews/bruise
ceiling/sealing
cent/scent/sent
chews/choose
cite/site/sight
colonel/kernel
cops/copse
days/daze
dear/deer
die/dye
doe/dough
earn/urn
ewe/yew/you
father/farther
fisher/fissure
great/grate
grosser/grocer
hair/hare

hear/here
idle/idol
jeans/genes
key/quay
knot/not
knows/nose/noes
liar/lyre
lode/load
meatier/meteor
mussel/muscle
one/won
ore/or
owed/ode
pail/pale
pair/pare/pear
paw/pore
paws/pause
pedal/peddle
plum/plumb
rains/reins/
   reigns
rapped/wrapped/
   rapt

rite/right/write/
   wright
roes/rows/rose
sell/cell
sighs/size
soul/sole
stake/steak
stalk/stork
suite/sweet
swayed/suede
tacks/tax
taught/taut
tea/tee
throne/thrown
toe/tow
vein/vain/vane
weak/week
whales/wails/
   Wales
which/witch
whole/hole
wrap/rap
yoke/yolk

THE E-CANCELLATION TEST

*   *   *

Some letters can be all but invisible in normal reading. Cross out all the letter "e"s in these short passages. Go straight through the passages; do not have second thoughts; do not go back or check your answers.

A. At the beginning of the twentieth century, there was a large farm near Los Angeles called the Hollywood Ranch. A few decades later, it was one of the most famous places in the world. The first movies were made in New York on the East Coast. But, as they used the light of the sun, the advantages of Los Angeles soon became apparent, where there were at least three hundred and fifty days of sun every year as well as picturesque natural scenery such as mountains, beaches and desert. After its heyday in the nineteen-thirties and nineteen-forties, Hollywood had to turn to television films before getting back to the blockbusters that dominate movie houses today. However, its position as the place that pro-duces most films has been overtaken by Bollywood in India.

B. Grace Paine lived in an isolated cottage for most of her life. In middle age she came to London and was astonished at city life. Best of all she loved her cooker with its row of controls. One day she told me about her amazing cooker. She had left her whole evening meal in the oven; at five o'clock the electric clock would switch it on and by seven a three-course meal would be ready to welcome her home. I almost envied her. But when we next met she related what had actually occurred: however automatic your cooker, you still have to remember to turn it on.

Answers and explanation are on page 154.

Answers and explanation are on page 154.

AMERICAN AND BRITISH STYLES OF SPELLING

*   *   *

In many cases American style has one spelling for a word, while British style has two (often with different meanings—"meter"/ "metre"). Many countries vary between the two styles, for example Australia and Canada.

American -or	British -our	Exceptions
color, favorite	colour, favourite	Am: glamour
American -old	**British -ould**	
mold, smolder	mould, smoulder	Am: shoulder
American -er	**British -re**	
center, theater	centre, theatre	Am: acre, ogre
American -ize	**British -ise**	
analyze, apologize	analyse, apologise	Brit: capsize, seize
American -se	**British -ce**	
defense, offense	defence, offence	Brit: advice/advise
American -og	**British -ogue**	
catalog, dialog	catalogue, dialogue	
American -ll	**British -l**	
fulfill, counsellor	fulfil, councillor	
American -e	**British -ae**	
feces, anemia	faeces, anaemia	

Inconsistent American and British spellings

ONDON CENTER COLLEGE

"Center" in London, England

University Square 4 Theatres

STARSK YAND HUTCH

"Theatres" in Madison, WI

American -l **British -ll**
jeweler, woolen jeweller, woollen

ONE-OFF DIFFERENCES BETWEEN WORDS

American	British	American	British
pajamas	pyjamas	karat	carat
skeptic	sceptic	sulfur	sulphur
tire	tyre/tire	jail	jail/gaol
check	cheque/check	ax	axe
disk	disc/disk	plow	plough
story	story/storey	whiskey	whisky
mustache	moustache		(Scotch)/
aluminum	aluminium		whiskey
z "zee"	z "zed"		(Irish)
		draft	draught/draft
		curb	curb/kerb

LO-COST GLAMO-NIT
Businesses and Products

* * *

Number-name spellings
> Turn 4 Pizza, 2 Hot 4 Ice, 4 Ever Nails, 4 Runners Only,
> Nails & Tan 4 U

Letter-name spellings
> B-secure Locksmiths, The Four Cs, Esso, Xpert Stationers,
> EXS, Just FX, Pow-R-Jac, Fax-U-Back Services

Initials
> Jaycee Fruits, Essanelle Hair, Emangee Clothing, Teecee
> Cleaners, Gee Jay's Pet Marts

Letter substitutions
> *"n" for "ng":* Stormin Records, Talkin' Loud
> *"n" for "and":* This 'N' That, Heads 'N' Extras, Plain n Fancy,
> Snip 'N' Shape, Chris 'N' Alice, Roots N Fruits
> *"ite" for "ight":* Northern Lite Scentsations, Nite-Cap Tavern,
> Hi-Lite Candles, Cut-Rite Barber Shop, Kleen Rite, Plumb
> Rite, Dee Lite Bakery, Girlz Nite Out
> *"hi" for "high":* Toyota Hi Lux, Hi-Power, Hi-Style, Hi Tec
> Autos, Hi-Spec Opticians
> *"lo" for "low":* Lo Cost Foodstores, Hilo Offset, Lospred
> *"flo" for "flow":* Flo-Rite, Crossflo, Doorflo, Freflo
> *"nu" for "new":* Nuchem, Nuvox Electronics, Nu Twist
> *"a" for "er/ar":* Betaware, ComputaTune, Mastascrew, Supa
> Shop, Supadriv, Supatravel, Solaglas Windscreens
> *"o" for "of":* Wood-O-Cork, Cleen-O-Pine, Rentokil
> *"o" for "or" or "our":* Flav-o-Lok, Glamo-Nit
> *"k" for "k/ck":* Krooklok, Hotpak, Bloc-Kote

1920s American examples (Louise Pound)
> Pret-O-Lite, Ra-dee-O, U All Kno After Dinner Mints,
> Uneeda Biscuit, Phiteezi Shoes, Rinkelaid, U-Rub-It-In

SERIOUS AND FRIVOLOUS
SPELLING REFORM

* * *

Classic Satire, Doubtfully Attributed to Mark Twain
In Year 1 that useless letter "c" would be dropped to be replased
either by "k" or "s," and likewise "x" would no longer be part of
the alphabet, apart from the kase of "ch," which will be dealt
with later. Year 2 might reform "w" spelling, so that "which"
and "one" would take the same konsonant, wile Year 3 might
well abolish "y" replasing it with "i" and Iear 4 might fiks the
"g/j" anomali wonse and for all.

Jenerally, then, the improvement would kontinue iear bai
iear with iear 5 doing awai with useless double konsonants,
and Iears 6–12 or so modifaiing vowlz and the rimeining voist
and unvoist konsonants. Bai Iear 15 or sou, it wud fainali bi
posibl tu meik ius ov thi ridandant letez "c," "y" and "x"—bai
now jast a memori in the maindz ov ould doderez—tu riplais
"ch," "sh," and "th" rispektivli.

Fainali, xen, aafte sam 20 iers ov orxogrefkl riform, wi wud
hev a lojikl, speling in ius xrewawt xe Ingliy-spiking werld.

Cut Spelling (CS) 1998
Som peple fear spelng reform wud mean spelng caos (as if
english spelng wer not alredy caotic). Th flexbility of th CS con-
cept minmizes that danjer. CS is not a rijid systm, but a
synpost pointng to th omission of redundnt letrs as th most
practicl and advntajus way of modrnizing english spelng.

Regularized Inglish, Axel Wijk, 1969
By the adoption ov such a system of spelling az Regulaized Inglish it wood be possible to lay down definit rules ov pronunciation for the Inglish language, which wood make it considerably
eazier for children to lern to read and write. In aul probability it
wood lead to a saving ov at least wun year's wurk for aul
scoolechildren.

THE "I" BEFORE "E" RULE

* * *

THE USUAL RULE: *"i" before "e" except after "c"*

Test it out on this sample.

1. recieve/receive
2. niece/neice
3. grief/greif
4. believe/beleive
5. wiegh/weigh

6. ceiling/cieling
7. sieze/seize
8. biege/beige
9. percieve/perceive
10. field/feild

Answers: "ie" words; 2 niece, 3 grief, 4 believe, 10 field; the rest are "ei" words.

The rule applies only when "ei" goes with long "ee" ("eel") not with the "ay" ("pay") sound of "beige" or with "ay" plus silent "g": "eight."

THE EXTENDED RULE: *"i" before "e" except after "c" when "ei" is said with a long "ee" sound*

However, there are still exceptions:
- some words have "ei" rather than "ie" despite having the long "ee" sound: seize, caffeine
- plural "-ies": currencies, policies; diphthongs: society, science; when "c" is said as "sh": sufficient, ancient

PERCENTAGE OF MISTAKES ON WEB PAGES

niece	8.7%	perceive	1.9%	caffeine	2.9%
deceive	2.5%	receive	1.8%	receipt	0.6%
conceive	2.3%	seize	1.7%	ceiling	0.3%

The only words with "cei" in their spelling in the top 5,000 for American English in the Brown corpus are: received, receive, receiving, ceiling, conceived, receives. Get these six right, and you won't need the rule very often.

OMG UR COOOOOOL
Chat Rooms
*   *   *

Mistakes
> suside, castore oil, mimick, dissapointed, attrack, masker-
> ade, potiential, meen to, saty awake, condeming, expecdency,
> sypathize, refering, removeing, carryoke

Initialese (see p. 95)
> lmnsbbo, OMG, brb, lol, bbl, gtg, rotk, nlol, thx, lmao, pm,
> ty, im, bf, alc, nyc, wtc, wtf

Leaving Out Vowels
> pls, ppl, mayb

Short Forms Common in Computer
Mediated Communication (CMC)
> u, ur, c, n, r, y, k, p

Expressing Extra Emotion
> hahahahah, soooooooooo complicated, awwwwww, hhehehe,
> helllloooo, haiiiiiiiii, naaahhh, grrrr shhhhhhhhhhh,
> heyyyyyyyyyyy, Pwoooohoooo, who is
> gayyyyyyyyyyyyyyyyyyyyyyyyyyyy??????????????????????????????,
> soooooooooooooooo coooooool, woohoo, excuuuuuuuse me
> plzzzzzz, backkkkkkkkkkkkkkkkkkkkk, lalalala, hugsssssss

Others
> wat is ya problem, lotsa, l8r, hai (hi), wafor, wots up, gawd,
> wassup, wat's up?, dat

Sample
> A: i like soundtracks more than real music.
> B: evil isnt always a bad thing
> C: how can evil not be bad lol
> C: that's why it's evil
> C: heheheh
> B: trust me . . .

A 2 B IN A KLASSY KAB
Taxicab Names

*   *   *

Letter names and number names

Y-Drive Taxis	E Z Taxi	Tony Xpress
L O Taxis	Go2 Cars	AirportLimo 2 Go
Xpressair	R-Cars	U-wana Taxi
Uneed	A2b Taxis	Xklusiv
Cabs 4 U	T4 Taxis	Cabs 4 Kids
Wair2 Travel	U Need A Taxi	

Puns

B-Line Taxis	Air & Back	Fareway Taxis
All-Ways Taxis		

Uses of "k" for "c"

McKab Taxis	Kiddie Kruises	Kipling Kab
Kwikasair	Kidz Karz	Klutch Kargo
Kwik Cars Ltd	Kazy's Cabs	
City Kabs	Klass Kars	

Initials

A.S.A.P. Taxis	Jay-Gees	P.D.Q. Taxis

Familiar novel spellings

Rite Taxi	Starlite Taxi	Air-n-Port Cars
Comfi Cars	Airport Carz	Top Flyte Taxi
Speedicars	Taxifone	
Out 'n About	Airports "R" Us	
Shuttle		

Others

Parceline	AL On Time	Bizzi Citiwide
Afaster Taxi	Kestral Taxis	Grabacab
Wideopen Air-	Supacars	1st Andycabs
n-Port Cars	Gaz Cabs	Cozy Cars

Excellancy	Aircomuter	ACAB
Happicabs	Luxecabs Ltd	Zed Cars
Air-Connex	Caffe De Taxi	Taxifast
Intime Private	HandiCabs	Bettacars
Hire	Ekco Taxi's	Exxtra's Limousine
Jeteck	Ms Taxi	Service
Croozer Cab	New-Moow Taxis	

HAS AMERICAN SPELLING IMPROVED?
The Lewis and Clark Diaries

* * *

These spellings are taken from the diaries of Meriwether Lewis, William Clark and their companions during their expedition from Mississippi to the West in 1804–1806.

Changes in Spelling Since 1806

—"c"+"k": publick, cholick/Chorlick/collick, Pacifick, Carthlick, musick

—double "l": barrell, devill, untill

—"-our": colour, labour, neighbouring

Variations on names

Sioux: Seouex, Shew, Soues, Sues, Soux, Scioues, Seaux, Souix

Pawnee: Pania, Paunees, pawne, ponies

Kansas: Caszes, Kances, Kanses, Kansis, Kanzus

Missouri: Mesury, Missor, Mussiry, Misoureis, Missourue, Missorea

Mistakes with Words with the Same Sound but Different Spelling (Homophones; see p. 40)

bare/bear, grate/great, pore/pour/poor, meat/meet, tale/tail, read/red, sore/saw, their/there, Greece/grease

Doubling or Not Doubling Consonants (see p. 96)

aproach, apeared, seting, midle, arival, imediately, submited, faithfull, maned (manned), verry, untill, aflicted, comming, oppinion, burried, flagg

Other Mistakes

dryed, ellegent, lieing, messinger, samon, swet, muddey, warr, beavour, rispect, previlege, nessy (necessary), behaveing, heavyly, purpendickler, destance, hickery, Pickture, buffalow/ buffaloe, trobelsom, Musquiters/Musquitoes/musquetoes/Musquitors, Roeing, adjasent, Warriers, butifull, Mockisons, Smallpoks, Instancetaniously

Source American Speech, 75, 2, 2000 & on-line diaries

FROM ADDILOU TO VSETIN

Spellings in Texan Place Names

* * *

The spelling of place names has always been much freer than the spelling of ordinary words. In North America they also reflect the languages of not only the incomers but also the indigenous inhabitants. Here are some of the more unusual Texas place names, taken from the Geographic Names Information System (GNIS). If you want to know how to pronounce them, ask a Texan.

Acebuche
Addielou
Bexar
Bieri
Calabazar
Chiltipin Creek
Chupadera Creek
Dreyfoos
Dyess
Echols Creek
Eylau Siding
Fertitta Lake
Fohn Hill
Gholson Creek
Gruhlkey
Gyp Canyon
Hlavacek Lake
Hopfs Creek
Ijams Lake

Iraan
Johhny Grave
   Mountain
Katemcy Creek
Keechi Creek
Lawhon Springs
Lazbuddie
Lotspelch School
Minjou Lake
Mulifest Creek
Okrob Heliport
Opdyke West
Opelika
Percilla
Psencik Cemetery
Quihi
Quitaque
Raab Spring
Romayor

Speegleville
Squier Cemetery
Tehuacana
   Cemetery
Thiebaud Dam
Tivydale
Uhland
Vahlasing Lake
Vrbas Lake
Vsetin
Whangdoodle Pass
Wied
XQZ Lake
Yokum
Yoledigo Creek
Yznaga
Zimmerhanzel
   Lake
Zummo

THE INTERNATIONAL
PHONETIC ALPHABET

* * *

The International Phonetic Alphabet (IPA) uses special letter symbols to show the pronunciation of any language, usually enclosing the transcript in slash marks / /. The number varies slightly from one accent of English to another, usually around 40. The following shows a version of IPA for General American English, with some alternatives sometimes found in American books (see Roca and Johnson, 1999, p. 190).

1. /ɪ/ bit	15. /ɔɪ/ boy	30. /ʒ/ or /ž/ genre
2. /ɛ/ red	16. /aʊ/ bout	31. /m/ mime
3. /æ/ fat	17. /p/ pip	32. /n/ noon
4. /ɒ/ lot	18. /b/ bob	33. /ŋ/ ring
5. /ʌ/ fun	19. /t/ tot	34. /tʃ/ or /č/
6. /e/ or /eɪ/ date	20. /d/ date	church
7. /ʊ/ good	21. /k/ kick	35. /dʒ/ or /ǰ/
8. /ɔ/ cloth	22. /g/ got	judge
9. /i/ sea	23. /f/ fine	36. /w/ wind
10. /ə/ about	24. /v/ vote	37. /h/ hot
11. /ɜ/ bird	25. /s/ cease	38. /j/ or /y/ yes
12. /o/ or /oʊ/ cone	26. /z/ zoos	39. /l/ lull
13. /u/ food	27. /ð/ the	40. /ɹ/ roaster
14. /aɪ/ bite	28. /θ/ think	
	29. /ʃ/ or /š/ shush	

Hamlet: /tə bi ɔɹ nɒ tə bi ðæt ɪz ðə kwɛstʃən
wɛðəɹ tɪz nobləɹ ɪn ðə maɪn tə sʌfəɹ
ðə slɪŋz ən æɹoʊz əv aʊtɹeɪdʒəz fɔɹtʃun
ən baɪ əpoʊzɪn ɛn ðəm/

ROCKIN' 'N' ROLLIN'
"-ing" and "-in"

* * *

The "-ing" in "taking," etc., can be said either as "ing" like "sing" or as "in" like "sin." The "in" pronunciation of "ing" is said to be more masculine and less formal. There is also a traditional association between "in'" and "huntin'" in the southern United States.

Advertising Slogans
Tennessee Sippin' Whiskey, LEXUS CATERS FOR THE HUNTIN', FISHIN', SHOOTIN' CLASS, finger lickin' good, I'm lovin' it

Song Titles by Sidney Bechet (New Orleans)
Sobbin' and Cryin', Walkin' and Talkin' to Myself, Laughin' in Rhythm, Slippin' and Slidin', Preachin' the Blues, Foolin' Me, Groovin' the Minor

Walkin' People
Walkin' Jim Stoltz (a wilderness walker), Beats Walkin' Western Swing Band, Always Walkin' Horse Locators, "Walkin' Down the Line" (Dylan song), *Walkin' the Dog* (Mosley book), Walkin' South (country music Web site)

Huntin' and Fishin'
Coon Huntin', Billy Bob's Huntin' n Fishin' (Gameboy game), the huntin, shootin, fishin brigade

Big truck tires, huntin', fishin', tractor pulls, country music, Charlie Daniels, and rebel flags are just a few words that might describe a redneck.

Don Marquis, *Noah an' Jonah an' Cap'n John Smith*
Noah an' Jonah an' Cap'n John Smith, . . .
Settin' up in Heaven, chewin' and a-chawin'
Eatin' their terbaccy, talkin' and a-jawin'; . . .

FROM ȝERE TO YEAR
Changing Letters of English

* * *

OLD ENGLISH (OE) *5th to 10th century A.D.*

ð **(eth)/þ (thorn)** = both voiced and unvoiced "th" (this/ theme): þe (the), þinȝ (thing), ðinȝ (thing), oðꞃe (other)

ȝ **"open" "g"** = spoken "g," "j" and a fricative no longer used: ȝǣꞅꞇ (ghost), ꝺæȝ (day), laȝu (law)

ƿ **(wynn, from runic alphabet)** = spoken "w": ƿiꝼ (wife), ƿæꞇeꞃ (water)

æ **(ash)** = spoken short or long "a": ꝼæꝺeꞃ (father), ꞅǣ ("sea"), æꞅc (ash)

letters used rarely in OE or as variants: x, k, q, z, g, j, v

little punctuation: low dot . = short pause; high ˙ = long

MIDDLE ENGLISH (ME) *11th to 15th centuries*

þ = spoken "th" in both forms (no ð): þat (that), þenk (think), deaþ (death); open top ʸ: ʸᵉ (the)

ȝ/g **"open"** ȝ = "j" ȝere (year); "closed": "g" = "g"; gere (gear), g after vowels = now lost fricative ryȝt (right)

letters used only as variants: u (for "v"), j (for "i")

punctuation: low . = short pause; ⸳ = medium; / = long

EARLY MODERN ENGLISH (EME) *16th to 17th centuries*

v/u one letter till about 1630 = spoken "v" or "u": vnkle, haue, vgly, receiue, giue, vnder, diuell, vs

i/j one letter till about 1640 = spoken "i" or "j": ioy, iudge, iigge, iackedaw, ieloosie, iniurie

ſ used in print for "s" until late 18th century long "s": ſoule, ſo, monſtrous, Paſſion, ſlaue, diſtraction

y/ie = interchanged medially in some words: myraculous, dye (die), nimph: "ie" finally in some words: Maie, heavie, eie

punctuation: ' = contraction, ? = question, ! = exclamation

FIFTEEN-YEAR-OLDS
AND SPELLING

* * *

TYPES OF ERRORS MADE BY 15-YEAR-OLDS

Insertion (adding letters)	untill/until	17%
Omission (leaving letters out)	occuring/occurring	36%
Substitution (replacing letters)	definate/definite	19%
"Grapheme substitution" (alternative sound-based spelling)	thort/thought	9%
Transposition (switching letters)	freind/friend	5%
Other		3%

MISTAKES BY 15-YEAR-OLDS IN TEN LINES OF WRITING

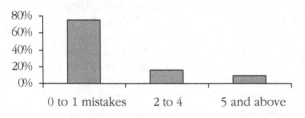

MISTAKES BY 15-YEAR-OLD BOYS AND GIRLS IN TEN LINES OF WRITING

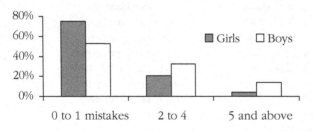

Source: Brooks et al. 1993

ORTHOGRAPHIC
REGULARITIES TEST

* * *

As well as the rules about how sounds connect to letters, English spelling also has many rules about which combinations of letters are allowed in a particular part of the word, called "orthographic regularities." None of the following is a real English word, but one word out of each pair is a *possible* word in that it conforms to these orthographic regularities. Check the possible words. Page 155 gives the answers and explanations.

1. blar/blarh
2. ckole/kole
3. leck/ckel
4. snove/snov
5. tcheb/cheb
6. chig/tchig
7. blic/blick
8. fanq/fanque
9. ster/sterh
10. gneit/teign
11. nowh/whon
12. flij/flidge
13. huz/huze
14. pluze/pluz
15. staj/stadge
16. truv/truve
17. whar/rawh
18. gnope/nope
19. dgain/jain
20. jarn/narj
21. blav/blave
22. gnil/lign/
23. lutch/tchul

24. nait/gnait
25. wras/sawr
26. qish/quish
27. quong/qong
28. lerh/rhell
29. forh/rhoff
30. smaze/smaz
31. sniv/snive
32. frak/frack
33. spiwh /spiw
34. plawh/plaw
35. terque/terq
36. squol/squl
37. dgoll/joll
38. klaze/klaz
39. nuft/gnuft
40. gewr/wreg
41. prew/prewh
42. nartch/ tcharn
43. plock/ploc
44. blive/bliv
45. wrof/fowr

Sources: Cook, 2004; Olson et al., 1985.

THE LETTERS OF THE ALPHABET
Richard Mulcaster, The Elementarie *(1592)*

*   *   *

E, besides the common difference of time and tune, is a letter of marvellous use in the writing of our tongue. . . . Which "e," though it be sometimes idly written, either of ignorance, if the writer be unlearned, and know not how to write, or of negligence, if he be learned, and mark not his hand, yet most times it is written to great purpose, even where it seems idle.

C is strong like to "k." before "a," "o," "u," either simple vowels, or combined in diphthongs, as *cankard, cautele, concord, coward, cunning,* or when it ends a foresyllable before any other consonant as "c" "q" "k" "t" as in *succede, acquaint, acknowledge, expecting.* "C," is weak like "s," before "e" and "i," either alone or in diphthong, as *cease, deceit, surcingle,* or before the qualifying silent "e," in the end, as *acceptance, whence, once.*

H is an aspiration, whose force before all vowels and diphthongs is easy to be perceived, as *Henrie, hunter.* . . .

O is a letter of as great uncertainty in our tongue, as "e," is of direction both alone in vowel, and combined in diphthong.

Q serves only in the nature of "k," or the strong "c," to go before the single or double "w," both consonantlike in force, and indifferent in place, as *quill, quail, . . . squint, squall, squat, squese,* or with the double "w," *qwail, acqwaint, qwik, . . .*

W The double "w" is a letter that hath accompanied our tongue from the original Germane, and is used sometimes as a vowel, sometimes as a consonant. It is never a vowel but in the diphthongs as, *draw, knew, throw, . . .*

X begins no English words, but ends many, as *wax, vex, yex,* and goes into the middle of their derivatives, as *waxing, vexeth, yexing,* and with the qualifying "e," *iaxe,* without *ax, pax, wax.*

Y likewise is sometimes consonantish, sometimes vowellish. Consonantish, when it leads a vowel, as, *yonder, young, . . .*

Z is a consonant much heard amongst us, and seldom seen . . .

NORRIF AND XIRYC
Dungeons and Dragons Names

*   *   *

To play D&D you have to have an appropriate persona. Here are some of the names of current players.

Agallela	Jeydrienne	Rehcran
Ahhzz	Johannixx	Rhomdruil
Astros	Kai-Raega	Shandakul
Bahagi	Kerahk	Shijin
Berdoingg	KouAidou	Slasiter
Boobooruboo	Leafgoodbread	Thyrwyn
Ceresco	Leariel	Tkolhoff
Chidebol	Legynd	uNtz!!
DaGreatJL	Loztastic	Vetrpger
Darvank	Lyferocks	Vrecknidj
Dhruin	Lynxara	Waqas
Ergazh	Mesclion	Welderd
Fallnwlf	Mysttic	Wyrmyone
Fraon	Nalancray	Xenobenzes
Gikar	Norrif	Xiryc
Gnarlo	Nyneve	Ynnep
Gnatetgnome	Oinkus	Zaxh
Griznuq	Oortoort	ZideX
H3llz Fire	Pneema	Zushoen
Hillelr	Raark	Zyguh
IkusaGwai	Ravenspoe	

BROCCOLI AND LETTUCE
History in Garden Plants

*   *   *

The spellings for plants grown have varied considerably over the years. (Dates from the *Oxford English Dictionary*.)

chili   chille (1662), chile (1676), chilli (1685), chili (1818)

daisy   dayeseye (1000), daysye, daysy, deysy, dasye, daizy

thyme   thyme (1398), tyme (1420), time (1563)

sunflower   sonne flower (1562), sunflow'r (1652), sunflower (1794)

squash   from Narragansett asquutasquash (1643)

okra   ocra (1707), ochre (1713), ockro (1750), okra (1777)

alyssum   alysson (1551), alasum (1840), alyssum (1876)

cabbage   cabache (1440), cabbyshe, cabidge, cabige, cabbach

lettuce   letuse (1290), lettuse, latewes, letews, letuce, lattice

garlic   garleac (1000), garleek, garlick [source: "gar" (spear) "leek"]

parsley   petersilie (1000), percil (originally Latin "petro" rock)

cucumber   cucumer (1382), cowcumber (1584), cucumber (1688)

cauliflower   cole florie (1597), cawly-flower, collyflower

peony   pioine (1265), pyone, piane, pyonie, piony, peiony

spinach   spynnage (1530), spenege, sippanage, spynach, spinech

pea   (originally "pease" was both singular and plural); pyse (1000), peose, pees, pes; (new singular) pea (1611)

onion   unyonn (1356), uniowns, oynyons, hunyn, oignion, ingyon

broccoli   broccoli (1699), brocoli (1732)

carrot   carette (1533), caret (1565), carrootes (1634)

REASONS FOR ODD SPELLINGS IN PLANT NAMES

1. *dialect variation in Middle English:* e.g., 15th century spellings of pease, pees, pease, pyson, pesone, peise, pese, peas

2. *borrowings from Latin and Greek:* chrysanthemum, gladiolus
3. *wrong ideas about word forms:* pease (singular, but changed to "one pea/two peas")
4. *plant names based on proper names:* dahlia (Dahl), fuchsia (Fuchs), poinsettia (Poinsett), wistaria (Wistar), cinchona (Chinchon)

TEST
British Versus American Newspapers

*   *   *

Which are British newspapers, which American?

1. . . . at the county's day labor hiring area, some workers
   said they might not be able to qualify for the program . . .
2. The sheer size of the voids would also allow visitors to
   experience something of the physical dimension of the
   trade center towers.
3. It makes no difference if they are real fur or fake, but it's
   worth checking that it won't moult too dramatically.
4. I've been eager to open up a dialog with Okrent.
5. Five-year-old Alyasa Klotz wanted a new wagon for Christmas.
6. THE QUICK actions of a Newquay mother helped save the
   life of her neighbour.
7. The FBI are hunting a bank robber who's struck eight
   times this year with only a pencil-drawn moustache as a
   disguise.
8. This Red Cross blood drive is also in honor of all public
   servants, past and present, who serve and protect every day.
9. The price of petrol at government stations in Iraq is about
   one cent per liter.
10. The LME launched its own internal investigation into alu-
    minium trading in August.
11. But if we look at the report through our skeptic's goggles,
    combined catalog and internet sales increased 11.4%.
12. New Doping Rules Favour GAA Cold Sufferers.
13. Most plums are preserved without the addition of sulfur
    dioxide, a chemical which causes an allergic reaction in
    some people.
14. Travelling people are being given cameras and training
    to document their lives, it was announced today.

Answers on page 156.

NO3ODY's $$$$s
Substitutes for Letters

* * *

Characters other than letters of the alphabet can stand in for letters, such as "@," "$," "£" and "+."

YE OLDE TUCK SHOPPE
Olde Tyme Spelling

*   *   *

The examples come from the United States, Australia, Ireland, Canada and the United Kingdom—Olde Tyme spelling affects all parts of the English-speaking world.
Some names go with genuinely old institutions, such as eighteenth-century pubs like "Ye Olde Admiral Rodney" in Cheshire. Others are modern "jokes": "Ye Ole Karaoke Web."

Around 1400 A.D. Middle English used the letter " Y " for "th" sounds in words like "this" and "think"; it resembled the modern letter "y." The word "the" was thus written as Yᵉ though

pronounced more or less as now. This letter " Y " became confused with the letter "y," so that "the" is written as "ye" in spelling that is supposed to look quaint. Other ways of suggesting antiquity are:

- **add an "e" at the end of words**, "olde," "shoppe," another holdover from Middle English where the "e" at the end of words like "love" was pronounced rather than silent.
- **use old-looking fonts**, Yᵉ Old Court Yard.
- **revive spellings once possible in English**, such as "fayre," used up to 1602, "tyme" up to 1552—though never with an

Yᵉ Olde Streete of LONDON Towne   "h" (the herb "thyme" has had an "h" since about

1500)—or "musick," used up to 1800. Usually the "antique" form is only one of the many possible alternative historic spellings. For example, "musique," "musyque," "musycque," "musik," "musyce," "musyk," "musicke," "musiq" all occurred in English.

Examples of Olde Tyme Spelling

Ye Olde Tuck Shoppe
The Publick Musick (group)
Ye Olde Admiral Rodney
Psychic Fayre
Ye Olde Cheshire Cheese Inn
Never Enough Thyme
    Shoppe
Ye Olde Chimney Sweeps
Thee Newe Worlde Inne
Ye Olden Days (Mickey Mouse
    film, 1933)
The Publick Theatre (Boston)
Ye Essex Baebes (medieval
    music singers)

MAGICK MUSICK
    MUSEUM
Ye Olde London Cab Hire
    Service
Olde Thyme Photographs of
    the Ladies of the House of
    Negotiable Affections
Ye Ole Karaoke Web
Olde Worlde Santas

OLDE WORLDE LACE
Ye Olde Tyme Radio Trading
    Post
Ye Olde Den of Iniquity
Olde Thyme Fayre
Ye Olde Directory Shoppe
Ye Olde Green Dragon
Wild River Pub and Publick
    House
Ye Olde Tea Shoppe
Olde Thyme Aviation
Ye Olde Trip to Jerusalem

Ye Olde Marquis
REAL FOOD

Ye Olde Slide and Popcorn
    Night
Ye Olde Fish & Chippe
    Shoppe
The University Towne House
Goose Fayre
Ye Olde George Inn
Olde Musick and Cokery
    Books
Ye Olde Crosse
Southampton Publick House
Ye Olde Soap Shoppe

HINTS ON PRONUNCIATION
FOR FOREIGNERS

*   *   *

This anonymous poem illustrating the problem words for English spelling has circulated constantly among teachers of English.

I take it you already know
Of *tough* and *bough* and *cough* and *dough*?
Others may stumble, but not you,
On *hiccough*, *thorough*, *lough* and *through*?
Well done! And now you wish, perhaps,
To learn of less familiar traps?
Beware of *heard*, a dreadful word
That looks like *beard* and sounds like *bird*,
And *dead*: it's said like *bed*, not *bead*—
For goodness sake don't call it *deed*!
Watch out for *meat* and *great* and *threat*
(They rhyme with *suite* and *straight* and *debt*).
A *moth* is not a moth in *mother*,
Nor *both* in *bother*, *broth* in *brother*,
And *here* is not a match for *there*
Nor *dear* and *fear* for *bear* and *pear*;
And then there's *dose* and *rose* and *lose*—
Just look them up—and *goose* and *choose*,
And *cork* and *work* and *card* and *ward*,
And *font* and *front* and *word* and *sword*,
And *do* and *go* and *thwart* and *cart*—
Come, come, I've hardly made a start!
A dreadful language? Man alive!
I'd mastered it when I was five!

DIRECTION OF WRITING

* * *

Arabic and Hebrew writing go from right to left; traditional Chinese and Japanese characters go from top to bottom. Does English go just from left to right? Signs from several English-speaking countries:

THY THIGH
The "th" Rule

*   *   *

The "th" combination of letters is pronounced in two different ways in "this" and "thistle." The "th" sound in "this" is "voiced," the sound in "thistle" is "unvoiced." The difference is the vibration from the vocal cords with the "th" in "this" but not with the "th" in "thistle." The pairs of words below differ chiefly by having one or other of these two sounds.

the	therapy	that	thatch	thou	thousand
there	theory	this	thistle	those	thong
their	theft	thus	thud	thence	theorem
them	thematic	than	thank	though	thought
these	thesis	then	Theo	thy	thigh

THE "TH" RULE
The words with voiced "th" like "the" and "than" are called "structure" words because they link words together in phrases—*"that* man with *the* beard."* The words with unvoiced "th" are ordinary nouns and verbs, etc., that need to be linked with structure words to make a phrase, called "content" words: "thesis," "thistle" and "thatch"—"the *thesis* about *thistles."*

EXCEPTIONS TO THE "TH" RULE
- words with silent "th": asthma, isthmus
- the structure word "through," said with unvoiced "th"
- words where "th" is pronounced "t": Thames, thyme, Thai
- pairs of nouns/verbs, etc., differing only over which "th" sound is used: bath/bathe, breath/breathe, wreath/wreathe, ether/either (for some people), loath/loathe, etc.

SNACK-TASTIC STEAK-O-RAMA
Word Endings
* * *

New words with unusual spellings are created by adding particular word endings.

tastic (presumably from "fantastic")

scan-tastic	Carb'Tastic	Snack-Tastic
friendstastic	*Tan-tastic!*	Rant-tastic!
cam-tastic	ghetto-tastic	Pop-tastic
Kid-Tastic	fat-tastic	Can-tastic

tacular ("spectacular")

Pet-tacular	crap-tacular	Snake-Tacular
Spa-Tacular	Mac-tacular	Pet'acular
Prank-tacular	Sports-tacular	

licious ("delicious")

paw-licious	madonnalicious	dinner-licious
soapylicious	Ice-A-Licious	Carb-O-Licious
picklelicious	spa-licious	Moolicious Dairy Bar
tea-licious	Soy-licious	

teria ("cafeteria")

Joke-a-teria	eat-a-teria	Gas-A-Teria
Snack-a-teria	wash-e-teria	Frame-a-teria
Disk-O-teria	Laugh-e-teria	wine-a-teria
book-a-teria	Dance-A-Teria	

delic

Shag-A-Delic	Dance-A-Delic	punk a delic
Funk-A-Delic	Mr.Sick-O'Delic	Pop-a-delic

Sci-fi-delic   Psy-Cow-Delic   Shop o Delic
psyk-E-delic   Cycle-Delic   glam-edelic
Rock-A-Delic   retro-delic

a/o-rama (originally from "panorama," invented in 1789)
Bounce-A-Rama   Putt-o-rama   Wood-o-rama
Blog-arama   Schlockorama   Swap-o-Rama
Elvis-A-Rama   Floor-O-Rama   Spell-o-rama
Liq-O-Rama   Beef-a-rama   Steak-O-Rama
Kleen-o-rama   Wig-o-rama   Stretch-O-Rama

SUPADUPA KILLAH MOBB
Hip-Hop Spelling
*   *   *

"Rebellious" novel spelling abounds in Hip-Hop, partly to show a way of speaking.

Hip-Hop Lyrics
Supadupa fly · Tell me whatcha gon do? · I'm in love wit chu · Rainbow Flava · it ain't nothin nobody can say cuz you're the one for me baby · they just wanna hold me Cuz im so supa · The rhythm on ya get yo groovin baby! · You know the old krumbsnatcha's in this land of decay · Got doe ma didn't know, good gracious alive! · Work 'til we break our back and you hear the crack of the bone to get by · my goals Just to stop smokin, and stop drinkin · Might of heard me spittin wit Cain and Fab playa · people killin people dyin children hurt and women cryin · Neva gave her tha cold shoulda' · if she's in the benz, I let her take ova' the Rova (vrrm-Vrrm!) · I ain't tryna wanna fight with ya man · IT PAYZ TO BE THA BOSS

Hip-Hop Chat
Ja wuss hip hop now he juss pop in mah opinion · I seriosly ain't heard one good verse from this kat · TUPAC IS DA GANG-STA OF DA SKY, HE WOULD ALWAYZ STAY IN MA HEART AS DA BEST RAPPER ONCE ALIFE · neva heard Busta diss a kat but his spit was hott · U hit it rite on the money dawg! · Killah Mobb 4 Life! · Who do u guyz think is the most Influencial Artist out of everybody? · even though he aint a artist u still gotta give respect to tha ONE AND ONLY

TEA-TIME OR TEATIME
OR TEA TIME?
Hyphens Joining Words

* * *

All the Words with Hyphens in the Brown Corpus of the
5,000 Most Frequent Words in American English

1. year-old	8. twenty-five
2. long-range	9. Bang-Jensen
3. over-all	10. full-time
4. so-called	11. anti-Semitism
5. long-term	12. Anglo-Saxon
6. part-time	13. middle-class
7. anti-trust	

Longest Hyphenated Word in the British National Corpus
oral-aggressive-anal-retentive-come-and-see-me-five-times-a-
week-for-years-at-vast-expense-or-how-do-I-know-you're-really-
committed (source: Leech et al., 2001)

CHANGES OVER TIME (*source:* Oxford English Dictionary)
Often a word changes over time from two words, "tea bag," to
one word with a hyphen, "tea-bag," to no hyphen, "teabag." The
form in boldface is the one given in *Webster's Unabridged*.

- week end 1638, **weekend** 1793, week-end 1970
- **won ton** 1948, won-ton 1952, wonton 1956
- **hot dog** 1908, hot-dog 1920
- **tea bag** 1898, tea-bag 1936, teabag 1977
- time-table 1820, time table 1838, **timetable** 1970
- **cooperate** 1616, co-operate 1762
- head maister 1576, **headmaster** 1776, head-master 1791
- screw driver 1779, **screwdriver** 1840, screw-driver 1842
- lamp shade 1850, lamp-shade 1877, **lampshade** 1960
- **air port** 1919, airport 1924
- **sight-see** 1824, sightsee 1913
- back stroke 1876, back-stroke 1908, **backstroke** 1958

TEST
Words That Are Commonly Misspelled

*   *   *

Circle the correct one.

1.	choize	choice	choise
2.	sincerely	sincerly	sincerelly
3.	thier house is . . .	there house is . . .	their house is . . .
4.	really	realy	reelly
5.	develope	divelop	develop
6.	kindergarten	kindegarten	kindergarden
7.	becuse	becase	because
8.	diffrint	different	diferent
9.	govemment	goverment	government
10.	busines affairs	busyness affairs	business affairs
11.	knowledge	noledge	nollidge
12.	profesional	professional	proffessional
13.	wold	wou'd	would
14.	I don't know where to go.	I don't know were to go.	I don't know wear to go.
15.	superseed	supercede	supersede
16.	address	adress	adresse
17.	cariere	carier	career
18.	accommodation	accomodation	acomodation
19.	particuler	particular	partikular
20.	intergrate	integrate	intigrate
21.	grammar	grammer	gramar
22.	descripe	describe	discribe
23.	begining	beginning	biginning
24.	interesting	intristing	intresting
25.	the book wich	the book which	the book witch

Answers are on page 157.

ALPHA BRAVO CHARLIE
Spoken Alphabets for English

* * *

For various military or police purposes, it is necessary to spell out crucial words, call signs or locations letter by letter in an unambiguous way over the radio or phone, etc. Two widely used variants are the "NATO" alphabet and the "Names" alphabet.

	NATO	*Names*
A	Alpha	Andrew
B	Bravo	Benjamin
C	Charlie	Charles
D	Delta	David
E	Echo	Edward
F	Foxtrot	Frederick
G	Golf	George
H	Hotel	Harry
I	India	Isaac
J	Juliet	Jack
K	Kilo	King
L	Lima	Lucy
M	Mike	Mary
N	November	Nellie
O	Oscar	Oliver
P	Papa	Peter
Q	Quebec	Queenie
R	Romeo	Robert
S	Sierra	Sugar
T	Tango	Tommy
U	Uniform	Uncle
V	Victor	Victor
W	Whiskey	William
X	X-ray	Xmas
Y	Yankee	Yellow
Z	Zulu	Zebra

Punning Shop Names

* * *

Bookshops
Bold Face Books
Hue-Man
Murder Ink

Apocalipsis
Rhythm & Muse

Plumbers
The Drain Surgeon
Lone Drainer and Pronto
Go with the Flow

Clog Busters
Royal Flush

Massage Therapists
A Kneaded Massage
Bodiwerks
Have Chair Will Travel

Tangible Results
A Touch of Class
Hands On Therapeutics

Delis
Crepe Vine
Love N Haught
Hugs & Quiches

Mega Bites
New Deli
Pasta T' Go-Go

Cafés and Coffeehouses
Uncommon Ground
Beanocchio
Bean There

Belly Good Cafe
Chock Full of Nuts
Grind N'brew

Boarding Kennels
Cat Calls
See Spot Run
Bark Avenue

Leash We Can Do
Citizen Canine
Barking Lot

Punning Shops and Restaurants from Different Countries

WHY ARE AMERICAN AND BRITISH STYLES OF SPELLING DIFFERENT?

* * *

The differences come from a small number of sources.

Noah Webster

Webster's 1828 *American Dictionary of the English Language* argued for:

"-or" rather than "-our": odour/odor. Webster blames Dr. Johnson for standardizing on "-our" in words like *favour* and *labour* rather than the traditional "-or."

"-er" rather than "-re": centre/center. Webster suggests returning to the earlier "-er" spelling in words like *centre*.

"-se" rather than "-ce": defence/defense. Webster's reasons for restoring the older "-se" to words like *defence* are partly the Latin sources, partly to make spelling uniform.

National Education Association, 1898

In 1898, the National Education Association in the United States of America listed twelve words that should be changed, namely:

> tho, altho, thru, thruout, thoro, thoroly, thorofare, program, prolog, catalog, pedagog, decalog.

While some have become American style ("program" and the "-og" words), others have not become standard written style even if they appear in informal contexts ("thru," "thorofare") (see p. 37).

HOW MANY WORDS ARE AFFECTED?

The only words affected by Webster's three main changes in the top 5,000 words of the Brown Corpus of American English are the following, plus their derivatives:

"-er":   center, theater, fiber

"-or":   labor, color, behavior, favor, honor, humor, liquor, neighbor, harbor

"-ize": realize, recognize, organize, authorize, characterize, emphasize but also "-ise" (Webster's): exercise, surprise (or surprize), enterprise, advise, arise, compromise
Other words in the top 5,000 that differ between American and British styles: program, tire, defense, license, jail, mold, wagon

CHEESE PATTER WITH ASIDES
Mistakes on Menus

* * *

OUR COUSINE
we serve food the taditional way . . . we would ike our patrons to order an entree per person · Traditional cousine · It's surpisingly filling · Experience Kyoto with tongue! · Open all days except on suday · we want your back

SNACKS AND APPERTIZERS
Toated Bagel · hand held breadfast · egg sandwiches garnished with luttuce · Hot Hors D'peivres · Gratinated snails · gourmet pig feet · herborized cheese · Shirimp Cocktail

APPETIZERS
Read Bean Soup with Lotus Seed · Bouilla Baisse · a teast of Olive oil · Egg Drip Soup · Oister soup · Ceasar salad · tuned salad

MAIN COURSES
fried wantons · whit-bean stew · unfrozen beef-rips · chilly chicken · Fried Port Chop · Buffer Dim Sum · Carmelized salmon fillet · Spicy and sour chestnet · Veal knee · prawns and brocolli in an oyster sauce · Seasonal veges · Western Ommelette · With sundried tomatoe salsa · scramble eggs · beef or fishdessert served with spicy ranch · sizzerling dishes

VEGETABLES
Chinese vegetables in space blend of white sauce · Served by itself or with two asides · Egg crocket groton style · Blanded tometos · Couliflower and Potato curry

ASSORTED DESERTS
Australian and imported cheese patter · Crape with fruit · decadent emulsion of sugar · Wide selection of daily cakes and

confectionary · The French chef of our shop made it hand-made dessert of it combines be prosperous and eat that and whatever.

DRINKS
Roze wine · Clab soda

TEST
Sounds or Letters?

* * *

Written English becomes so much part of our lives that it has an effect on how we *hear* spoken English. People sometimes "hear" sounds because they know the letters in the word. To see how you are affected by this, quickly count how many *sounds* there are in each of the following words.

1. bought ___	18. music ___	35. rich ___
2. box ___	19. judge ___	36. wing ___
3. thin ___	20. who ___	37. page ___
4. him ___	21. spend ___	38. unit ___
5. catch ___	22. age ___	39. me ___
6. the ___	23. it ___	40. cost ___
7. chop ___	24. think ___	41. she ___
8. crash ___	25. match ___	42. crop ___
9. of ___	26. chat ___	43. shock ___
10. edge ___	27. next ___	44. bat ___
11. fix ___	28. thought ___	45. let ___
12. do ___	29. land ___	46. trust ___
13. then ___	30. nothing ___	47. back ___
14. broccoli ___	31. ought ___	48. stamp ___
15. jet ___	32. win ___	49. past ___
16. light ___	33. stupid ___	50. washing ___
17. job ___	34. plant ___	

Answers on page 158.

HIGH KLASS SHOPS
Unusual Spelling in Shop Names

* * *

THE GHASTLY KHAKI WALTZ
Unusual English Spellings

* * *

"pph" = "f": sapphire, Sappho
"cch" = "ch," zucchini; = "k": gnocchi, Pinocchio, saccharine
"ch" = (silent), yacht, Crichton; = "sh," fuchsia (though derived
  from Leonard Fuchs)
"dh" = "d": dhobi, Gandhi, dhoti, dhall, dhow, dhurrie, jodhpur
"kh" = "k": khaki, khan, Khmer, sheikh, Sikh, Khyber
"rrh" = "r": diarrhea, hemorrhage, cirrhosis; (silent): catarrh,
  myrrh
"ae" = "air": aerial; = "ee": Caesar
"ltz" = "s": waltz; = "ts": seltzer, schmaltz
"ea" = "eh": great, break, steak, Yeats
"rtz": quartz, Hertz
"rgh" = "rg": sorghum, burgher, Pittsburgh
"gn" (initial)= "n": gnu, gneiss, gnostic, gnat, gnaw, gnome
"sth" = "s": asthma, isthmus
"gu" = "gw": guano, Guinevere
"gm" = "m": phlegm, paradigm, diaphragm
"th" = "t": thyme, Thames, Thompson, Thomas, Esther
"oeu": hors d'oeuvres
"mn" = "m": autumn, column, condemn, damn, solemn, hymn
"ieu" = "you": adieu, lieu
"gh" = "g": ghost, ghastly, Ghana, gherkin, ghetto, ghoul
"cz" = "s": Czar; = "tch": Czech
"ez" = "eh": chez, rendezvous, laissez-faire
"rr" = finally: burr, err, shirr

SOME ONE-OFF WORDS
djinn, chamois ("shammy"), junta ("hunta"), colonel, Xhosa
("hosea"), England/English ("ingland/inglish"), of ("ov"), milieu
("mealyer"), ache ("ehk")

TRAFFIC SIGNS FROM
SEVERAL COUNTRIES

* * *

WELCOME COMPLIMENTS
Two Common Mistakes

*   *   *

Compliment = a remark intended to praise or please
Complement = something that fills up or completes (*Webster's*)

Complimentary Food

Dinners are complimented with the appropriate condiments.

Rosettes of Smoked Norwegian Salmon complimented with a duo of Relishes

Mouthwatering flavors of red raspberry, currant, plum jam and raisins are complimented by spicy pepper and herb notes.

Enjoy a complimentary pastry when ordering any hot beverage.

No dessert menu is complete without Ice cream though, so we have chosen a variety of fabulous flavours to compliment the menu.

Complex with a good balance of ripe berry flavors, low acidity & soft tannins complimented by a long finish.

Other Compliments

. . . full time teachers . . . are complimented by highly respected part time teachers from the business community.

Luxuriant tropical gardens and attractive landscaping are complimented by the tall palms and majestic flamboyant trees.

NATO and the EU army are complimentary, not competitive.

The bedroom is complimented by a king sized brass bed.

Wellcome to My Web Page

    Wellcome to Bavaria (wellcome to yodelling area).
    Hopefully we can soon wellcome you here again.
    Wellcome to Life, Wellcome to Geneva
    Scarecrow grapevine wreath will give a warm wellcome!
    Wellcome I really want to know that is your opinion.

Various people, objects and shapes can be used as letters.

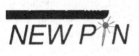

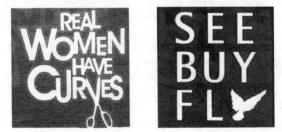

SHAKESPEARE AND SPELLING

*   *   *

Shakespeare's Name
All these spellings for Shakespeare—the writer rather than other people with the same name—are found before 1616, the year of his death:

Shakespeare, Shake-speare, Shakspeare, Shaxberd,
Shakespere, Shak-speare, Shakspear, Shakspere, Shaksper,
Schaksp., Shakespear, Shakespheare.

To Be or Not to Be
The Tragedie of Hamlet First Folio, 1623, original spelling (not necessarily Shakespeare's), using the long "s" ſ used by English printers in the seventeenth and eighteenth centuries.

To be, or not to be,that is the Queſtion :
Whether 'tis Nobler in the minde to ſuffer
The Slings and Arrowes of outragious Fortune,
Or to take Armes againſt a Sea of troubles,
And by oppoſing end them : to dye,to ſleepe
No more ; and by a ſleepe, to ſay we end
The Heart-ake, and the thouſand Naturall ſhockes
That Fleſh is heyre too? 'Tis a conſummation
Deuoutly to be wiſh'd. To dye to ſleepe,
To ſleepe, perchance to Dreame; I, there's the rub,
For in that ſleepe of death, what dreames may come
When we haue ſhuffel'd off this mortall coile,
Muſt giue vs pawſe

Different versions of this speech are on page 131.

Other Familiar Quotations from the First Folio of Hamlet
- There are more things in Heauen and Earth, *Horatio*,
  Than are dream't of in our philoſophy
- Something is rotten in the State of Denmarke.
- Goodnight ſweet Prince,
  And Flights of Angels ſing thee to thy reſt

SPELLING GAMES
Set 2

*   *   *

Matching Letters
Each of two players writes down a six-letter word, say,
C O M M O N

The aim is to discover the other person's word. Each player
produces another six-letter word, say O R I G I N

They score one point for each letter that is in *exactly* the same
place in the target word, in this case I for the last letter, N.
Repeat until the word is found. Proper names and plurals are
not allowed for the target word but can be used in the test
words. A four-letter version of the same game can be played by
two people in a car.

Last and First
The aim is to supply a word of the appropriate category that
begins with the last letter of the preceding word. So if players
choose countries as a category, the sequence might be:

Japan > Nigeria > Afghanistan > New Zealand > . . .

Players lose a point when they cannot supply a word.

I Love My Love with an A
Each player describes his or her love with words starting with a
given letter of the alphabet, following the formula:

I love my love with an A because she is Athletic. I hate her
with an A because she is Artful. Her name is Amanda and
she comes from Alaska.

Players go through the letters of the alphabet: X, Y and Z are
optional. This game goes back at least to Samuel Pepys (1669).

BANANNAS FOR BREKFAST

* * *

Handwritten notices in streets and on blackboards, doors, etc., are prone to error.

THE EIHGTEEN-MILLION-DOLLAR SUPPRISE

* * *

Here are specimen spelling mistakes from 75 versions of the spam e-mail inviting you to accept millions of dollars. These may, of course, be deliberate attempts to appear naive or to evade spam detectors.

The Preamble
YOU MAY BE SURPRISE TO RECEIVE THIS LETTER • I ONLY GOT YOUR CONTACT ADDRESS FROM INDISCREET SEARCH

The Money
THE SUM OF EIHGTEEN MILLION UNITED STATE DOLLARS (US$18,000,000,00.)

The Background
THE CHAIRMAN . . . IS NOW HIDDING IN A FORIEGN COUNTRY • he fore saw the looming danger in Zimbabwe • he was shoot by hired killers • many people in other state knows on what this perpatrate against christian • [my cancer] has defiled all forms of medical treatment • you will understand my plige

Your Involvement
you will advice on areas of investment • At this time I can not devulge further information • WE HAVE BEEN RELIABLY INFORMED OF YOUR DISCRETENESS

Legal Arrangements
my words is my bond • I will involve my confidant lawyer • once the layer have your consent and trust then he can proceed immediately • the funds will be donated to a discreted trust fund for the purchase of arms and amunnitions

An Alternative Type of Spam

Hello,I finlaly was able to lsoe the wieght I havebeen sturggling to lose for years!And I couldn't bileeve how simple it was!Amizang pacth makes you shed the ponuds!It's Guanarteed to work or your menoy back

ROCK 'N' ROLL 'N THIS 'N THAT

* * *

The letter "n," with or without an apostrophe, can stand for "and," as in *rock n roll*, particularly in shop names and signs—in fact, simply an approximation to a common spoken form.

ROCK 'N' ROLL 'N THIS 'N THAT

* * *

Food 'n' Drink

Bacon, Scrambled Egg 'n Toast
Burgers: Cheddar 'n Bacon:
 Mushroom 'n Swiss;
 BBQ 'n Bacon
Free -n- Cool
French Toast 'n Syrup
IN-N-OUT Burger

Lunch 'n Dinner
Pancakes 'n Syrup
Soups n Sides
Steak n Shake
Surf 'n Turf Burger
Thin 'n crispy fries

Pairs or Groups of People

Amos 'n' Andy
Bone thugs-n-harmony
Chip N Dale

Guns N Roses
Hoof 'N Horn
Salt 'N' Pepa

Shop Names, etc.

Bellsnwhistles
Birds n Ways
Books 'n' Bytes
Cherubs-N-Chocolate
Coon 'n Crockett Muzzleloaders
 Club
Crochet 'N' More
Dark 'n Dazed
Eat 'n Park
Fast 'n' Bulbous Music Webzine
The Food~n~More Food Ring
Heat-N-Glo
Hitch n Hike—The Climbing
 Shop
Kash n' Karry Food Stores
Kibbles 'n Bits dog food
Kids 'n cars
Linens 'n Things
Love-n-Kisses

Mains 'N' Drains
Memphis Rock 'n' Soul
 Museum
Nose-N-Toes Llama Gifts
Oaks 'n' Folks Newsletter
Pick 'n Pay
Print-n-play toys
The Rock 'n' Bowl store
Show-n-Tell
Ski-N-Ride
Spic 'N' Span
Steak n Shake
Sun 'n Fan
Swing-N-Slide
This N That
Wet 'n Wild
Whim 'n Rhythm 2003
Wings N' Things Exotic
 Bird Supply

MARK TWAIN
Payment by the Word

*   *   *

. . . At that time I was scrambling along, earning the family's bread on magazine work at seven cents a word, compound words at single rates, just as it is in the dark present. I was the property of a magazine, a seven-cent slave under a boiler-iron contract. One day there came a note from the editor requiring me to write ten pages—on this revolting text: 'Considerations concerning the alleged subterranean holophotal extemporaneousness of the conchyliaceous superimbrication of the Ornithorhyncus, as foreshadowed by the unintelligibility of its plesiosaurian anisodactylous aspects.'

Ten pages of that. Each and every word a seventeen-jointed vestibuled railroad train. Seven cents a word. I saw starvation staring the family in the face. I went to the editor, and . . . I said, 'Read that text, Jackson, and let it go on the record; read it out loud.' He read it: 'Considerations concerning the alleged subterranean holophotal extemporaneousness of the conchyliaceous superimbrication of the Ornithorhyncus, as foreshadowed by the unintelligibility of its plesiosaurian anisodactylous aspects.'

I said, 'You want ten pages of those rumbling, great, long, summer thunderpeals, and you expect to get them at seven cents a peal?'

He said, 'A word's a word, and seven cents is the contract; what are you going to do about it?'

I said, 'Jackson, this is cold-blooded oppression. What's an average English word?'

He said, 'Six letters.'

I said, 'Nothing of the kind; that's French, and includes the spaces between the words; an average English word is four letters and a half. By hard, honest labour I've dug all the large words out of my vocabulary and shaved it down till the average is three letters and a half. I can put one thousand and two hundred words on your page, and there's not another man alive that can come within two hundred of it. My page is worth eighty-four dollars to me. It takes exactly as long to fill your magazine page with long words as it does with short ones— four hours. Now, then, look at the criminal injustice of this requirement of yours. I am careful, I am economical of my time and labour. For the family's sake I've got to be so. So I never write "metropolis" for seven cents, because I can get the same money for "city." I never write "policeman," because I can get the same price for "cop." And so on and so on. I never write "valetudinarian" at all, for not even hunger and wretchedness can humble me to the point where I will do a word like that for seven cents; I wouldn't do it for fifteen. Examine your obscene text, please; count the words.'

He counted and said it was twenty-four. I asked him to count the letters. He made it two hundred and three.

I said, 'Now, I hope you see the whole size of your crime. With my vocabulary I would make sixty words out of those two hundred and five letters, and get four dollars and twenty cents for it; whereas for your inhuman twenty-four I would get only one dollar and sixty-eight cents. Ten pages of these sky-scrapers of yours would pay me only about three hundred dollars; in my simplified vocabulary the same space and the same labour would pay me eight hundred and forty dollars. I do not wish to work upon this scandalous job by the piece. I want to be hired by the year.' He coldly refused. I said:

'Then for the sake of the family, if you have no feeling for me, you ought at least to allow me overtime on that word extemporaneousness.' Again he coldly refused. I seldom say a harsh word to any one, but I was not master of myself then, and I spoke right out and called him an anisodactylous plesiosaurian conchyliaceous Ornithorhyneus, and rotten to the heart with holophotal subterranean extemporaneousness. God forgive me for that wanton crime; he lived only two hours.

Mark Twain, Speech to the Associated Press, 1906

LOL AND KISS IN THE CHAT ROOM

* * *

Most chat room forms use the first letters of a phrase—JAM (just a minute). Many are traditional novel spellings predating the Internet—TTFN (ta-ta for now) or TANSTAAFL (there ain't no such thing as a free lunch). Some use the letter-name convention—CUL8R (see you later)—found in text messages and pop groups.

AFAIK as far as I know
AFK away from keyboard
AISI as I see it
ASAP as soon as possible
A/S/L age/sex/location
BBL be back later
BCNU be seeing you
B4 before
BF boyfriend
BFN 'bye for now
BTU back to you
BTW by the way
C2C cheek to cheek
CUS see you soon
FITB fill in the blanks
F2F face to face
FWIW for what it's worth
FYI for your information
GAL get a life
GFC going for coffee
GL good luck
GR8 great
H&K hugs and kisses
HB hurry back
IC I see
IMO in my opinion
IOW in other words

IRL in real life
ITA I totally agree
JAM just a minute
J2LUK just to let you know
KISS keep it simple, stupid
KIT keep in touch
L8R later
LOL laughing out loud
NP no problem
OIC oh, I see
OTL out to lunch
OTOH on the other hand
PLZ please
P2P person to person
RSN real soon now
RUOK are you OK?
SWIM see what I mean?
TANSTAAFL there ain't no such thing as a free lunch
TOY thinking of you
TTFN ta-ta for now
TTYL talk to you later
TY thank you
WB welcome back
YBS you'll be sorry
YW you're welcome

RULES FOR DOUBLING CONSONANTS

*   *   *

Many spelling mistakes reveal problems with consonant doubling, sometimes putting a superfluous consonant in, sometimes leaving one out:

accomodate	finnished	tradditional
beginers	occassion	usefull
controlls	profficiency	
corect	refering	

Second-language users of English make similar mistakes:

allmost	bussiness	oppinion
arived	carefull	peper
biger	comming	sory
bigginer	monney	sucessful

A CONSONANT-DOUBLING RULE

Most single written vowels, "a e i o u," correspond to two different spoken vowels—short, checked vowels as in "Dan," "den," "din," "don," "dun," versus long "free" vowels as in "Dane," "Venus," "fine," "bone," "dune." Many of the complexities of English spelling concern which vowel is involved. An "e" following the consonant shows that the preceding vowel is the long one of the pair (p. 121): "bate/bat," "rune/run." A double consonant, on the other hand, shows that the vowel has a "short" pronunciation—the "a" in "laddy"—rather than a "long" pronunciation—the "a" in "lady."

"**a**" laddy/lady, planning/planing, latter/later
"**e**" better/beta, dilemma/scheme, essence/thesis
"**i**" winner/whiner, bitter/biter, ridding/riding
"**o**" lobby/lobe, hopping/hoping, dotted/doted
"**u**" supper/super, rudder/ruder, hugger/huger

- a few words have unexpected "long" vowels before double consonants: ball, small, all, staff, class, furry
- some consonants take an extra letter rather than doubling: "lack" versus "lake," "cadge" versus "cage"
- some consonants never double (or rarely): "h," "j," "k" (trekking), "q," "v" (revving), "w," "x," "y"
- American and British styles of spelling have some differences in doubling, "travelling/traveling," though British style often allows both forms

---

British and American Styles of Consonant Doubling

	British Style	American Style
Single versus double "l"	appal	appall
	enrolment	enrollment
	skilful	skillful
	travelling	traveling
	jeweller	jeweler
	woollen	woolen
Words ending in "p"	kidnapped	kidnapped
	worshipped	worshipped
Single versus double "g"	wagon, waggon	wagon

Commonest words with doubling for each letter (top 5,000 words in the Brown Corpus):

    (aa), Bobby, according, added, been, off, suggested, (hh), (ii), (jj), B'dikkat, all, community, cannot, too, support, (qq), carried, less, little, vacuum, (vv), (ww), (xx), (yy), jazz.

Note: the Brown Corpus used science fiction books, hence it includes words like "B'dikka't" (Cordwainer Smith) and "grokked" (Robert Heinlein).

Vowels that rarely double

    "a" (Isaac, Saatchi), "i" (skiing, Hawaiian), "u" (vacuum, continuum)

GROBAL BUSSINESS
Mistakes by Nonnative Speakers

* * *

Words most commonly misspelled by overseas students
accommodating, because, beginning, business, career, choice, definite, develop, different, describe, government, integrate, interest(ing), kindergarten, knowledge, life, necessary, particular, professional, professor, really, study/student, their/there, which, would

Some typical mistakes
because: beaucause, becase, becaus, becouse, becuase
address: adres, adress, adresse
business: busines, bussines, buisness, bussiness
professional: profesional, professinal, proffessionall
sincerely: sinarely, sincerelly, sincerley, sincersly
student, etc.: studet, stuienet, studing, studyed, stuent

Mistakes by speakers of different languages
Arabic: changed vowels: obundant; or added vowels: punishement
Chinese: consonants omitted: subjet; addition of "e": boyes
French: doubling: comming; vowel substitution: materiel
German: "e" left out: happend; change of "i" for "e": injoid
Greek: consonant change, "d/t": Grade Britain; "c/g": Creek
Japanese: added vowels: difficulity; "l"/"r": grobal, sarari

GUESS THE FIRST LANGUAGES

1. Gambridge	8. familly	15. telefon
2. reseption	9. calld	16. secondaly
3. proffessional	10. photoes	17. defacult
4. vocaburaries	11. endiveduoly	18. revoluzion
5. mentionned	12. monney	19. subejects
6. addresse	13. particulery	20. leccons
7. rutine	14. enthousiastic	21. tink (think)

Answers on page 159.

UNIQUE NEW YORK
Tongue Twisters or Eye Twisters?

* * *

Tongue twisters demonstrate the variety of letters that correspond to particular sounds of English. They may be as difficult to read as to say. Deaf students have problems with tongue twisters despite not being able to hear them (Hanson, Goodell and Perfetti, 1991). Usually the short twisters have to be repeated several times.

- Rubber baby buggy bumpers
- Six thick thistle sticks
- Green glass gas globe
- Peggy Babcock
- Miss Smith's fish sauce shop seldom sells shell fish
- Double dozen durable damask dinner doilies
- Old oily Ollie oils oily automobiles
- He ran from the Indies to the Andes in his undies
- Any noise annoys an oyster but a noisy noise annoys an oyster most
- A cup of proper coffee in a proper coffee cup
- Can you imagine an imaginary menagerie manager imagining managing an imaginary menagerie?
- You can have fried fresh fish, fish fresh fried, fresh fried fish, or fresh fish fried

- A regal rural ruler
- Red leather, yellow leather
- Which wrist watches are Swiss wrist watches?
- Is there a pleasant peasant present?
- The dude dropped in at the Dewdrop Inn
- Who washed Washington's white woolen underwear when Washington's washer-woman went west?
- Shave a cedar shingle thin
- Unique New York
- A thin little boy picked six thick thistle sticks
- I'm not the pheasant plucker, I'm the pheasant plucker's mate, and I'm only plucking pheasants 'cause the pheasant plucker's late

MAKING ENGLISH BETTER
Spelling Reform

* * *

Here are some of the revisions to English spelling that have been suggested, known as "spelling reform."

Harry Lindgren (1969): *Spelling Reform Step 1 (SR1):* the short "e" sound should always be spelled as "e": eny, meny, frend, hed, welth, wether, sed, ses, relm, redy

John Cheke (1542): *double "aa" for long "a" and omission of silent "e":* maad, straat, aag, aal, aancient, aapril, aac, waav, taap

Noah Webster (1828): *delete "u" from "-our" (the source of American-style "-or"—perhaps the only successful reform):* color, harbor, rumor, vapor, favor, odor, labor

John Hart (1569): *get rid of "y," "w," "c" and silent "e":* mi, kall, los

Axel Wijk (1959): *regularize irregular forms:* woz, laafter, enybody, thare, tauk, choze, luvd, scoole

Cut Spelling *(advocated by the Simplified Spelling Society):*

Rule 1: *Cut letters irrelevant to the sound:* hed (a), ajust (d), frend (i), peple (o), rite (w), fech (t)

Rule 2a: *Cut unstressed vowels before L/M/N/R:* womn (a), systm (e), victm (i), mountn (ai), glamr (ou), etc.

Rule 2b: *Cut vowels in regular endings:* likd, liks, likng, likbl

Rule 3: *Write most double consonants single:* ad, wel, botl, hopd, hopng, acomodate

Substitute letters:
- "f" for "gh" and "ph": ruf, fotograf, tuf, cuf, graf
- "j" for "soft" "g": jin, juj
- "y" for "igh": sy, syt, syn

Use fewer capitals and apostrophes:
- only proper names have capitals: France/french, Paris/parisian
- apostrophes only to link words: she'd, it's, we'l, let's, oclok, hadnt, Bils hous

YERTLE THE TURTLE
Names in Dr. Seuss Books

*   *   *

Biffer-Baum Birds	Grickily Gractus	Rink-Rinker-Fink
Bippo-No-Bungus	Grinch	Skritz
Bloogs	Ham-ikka-Schnim-	Sneetches
Brown Bar-ba-loots	ikka-Schnam-	Snuvs
Bumble-Tub Club	ikka-Schnopp	Thnadners
Chief Yookeroo	Herk-Heimer	Thwerll
Chippendale Mupp	Sisters	Uncle Ubb
Chuggs	High Gargel-orum	Vrooms
Collapsible Frink	Humpf-Humpf-a-	Wily Walloo
Dawf	Dumpfer	Wumbus
Dr. Spreckles	Jill-ikka-Jast	Yekko
Fiffer-feffer-feff	Klotz	Yertle the Turtle
Flunnel	Kwigger	Yottle
Foo-Foo the Snoo	Long-Legger	Yuzz-a-ma-Tuzz
Foona-Lagoona	Kwong	Zable
Baboona	Nazzim of Bazzim	Zizzer-zazzer-zuzz
Fuddnudler	Nooth Grush	Zlock
Brothers	Nutch	
Glotz	Quimney	

Checking how common these spellings are against a large sample of English shows:

tz: Glotz—a handful of words end in "tz" such as "blitz"

wf: Dawf—no words end in "wf"

kw: Kwong—no English words start with "kw"

skr: Skritz—the only BNC word starting with "skr" is "skrew"

kk: Jill-ikka-Jast—the only words with "kk" are "trekking/trekker"

vs: Snuvs—the only words ending in "v" are "rev," "spiv" and "lav"

rll: Thwerll—no words have "rll"

GURANTEED APPARTMENTS
Mistakes on Painted Signs

*   *   *

184
MAGDALON ST.

CRAFTCo
CRAFTS
CARDS T-SHIRTS HATS & clothes
SILK SCARFES & TIES
POTTERY
J.E.Wellery
PAINTED FABRIC
PRINTS WOOD
CLOCKS GLA TOYS and
GARDEN SCULPTURE POTS
AUTOMATIONS

THE SNOOTY FOX
• Fine Wines, Cask Ales
  & Crazy Cocktails
• RETRO Vynal Juke box

Avanced Warning

Trafalgar Square Closed

CAN COMPUTERS LEARN
ENGLISH SPELLING?

* * *

A computer programmed to acquire English spelling produced the following suggestions for how to pronounce words.

ache	atch	mow	my
angst	ondst	nymph	mimf
beau	bjew	ouch	aitch
blithe	blit	plaid	played
breadth	brebt	plume	plom
brooch	brutch	queue	kwoo
chew	chw	scarce	skers
czar	vor	sphinx	spinks
dose	dose	spook	spuk (as in book)
dreamt	dremp	suede	swede
ewe	woo	svelte	swelt
feud	flued	taps	tats
garb	gorg	tsar	tar
gin	(be)gin	womb	wome
hearth	horse	zip	vip
lewd	lead		

The errors came to only 2.7% of the total words the computer "learned."

CORRECTING HUMAN MISTAKES
The person entering the words into the computer sometimes typed them wrong. This is what the computer made of them.

Target Word	Human Mistake	Computer Correction
chaise	chez	chays
dang	dayng	dang
fold	rold	dold
skull	skool	skull

HISTORY TEST

*   *   *

Put these passages into the order in which they were written. Letter forms have been modernized.

A   Hauing spent many yeeres in studying how to liue, and liu'de a long time without mony: hauing tired my youth with follie, and surfetted my minde with vanitie, I began at length to looke backe to repentaunce, & addresse my endeuors to prosperitie: But all in vaine, . . .

B   I think that the main task for intellectuals, aside from resistance to repression and violence, is to try to articulate goals, to try to assess, to try to understand, to try to persuade, to try to organise.

C   Spare neither Pains or Expence to gain all possible Intelligence on your March, to prevent Surprizes and Accidents of every Kind, and endeavour, if possible, to correspond with General Schuyler, so that you may act in Concert with him.

D   Let that vast number of Gentlemen which have made their compositions for syding with him in his unjust and destructive Warres at Goldsmiths hall, speak or be silent, whose Wives and Children, live in want, and happily not without tears enough for the indigence whereunto they are reduced through his only means.

E   During a portion of the first half of the present century, and more particularly during the latter part of it, there flourished and practised in the city of New York a physician who enjoyed perhaps an exceptional share of the consideration which, in the United States, has always been bestowed upon distinguished members of the medical profession.

F   Yn Brytayn buth meny wondres. . . . The secunde ys at Stonhenge bysydes Salesbury. Thar gret stones and wonders huge buth arered an hyg, as it were gates so that that semeth gates yset upon other gates.

Answers on page 159.

SPELLING GAMES
Set 3

*   *   *

Ghosts

Ghosts can be played by any number of people from two upward. The object is never to finish a word.

1. The first player thinks of a word longer than two letters and writes the first letter: b
2. The next player has to continue a possible word by supplying the next letter he or she thinks is in the word: br
3. The round continues till a player completes a word longer than two letters: bread
4. At any time other players can challenge whether there is really a word with that spelling. If the player who gave the letter cannot supply one, they become a third of a ghost; if they supply a word, the challenger becomes a ghost.
5. After a player loses three times, he or she becomes a complete ghost and does not take part in the rest of the game.
6. The player who is not eliminated wins.

A variant on this called *Superghosts* allows players to add letters at the beginning and in the middle of words, for example:

t > tr > ttr > uttr > utter

Another variant makes ghosts invisible so that living beings who talk to them become ghosts themselves. For a full account, see the works of James Thurber.

The Parson's Cat

In each round, players describe the parson's cat with an adjective starting with a given letter, going through the alphabet in order.

> The parson's cat is an angry cat . . .
> The parson's cat is a brainy cat . . .
> The parson's cat is a cheeky cat . . .
> The parson's cat is a deceitful cat . . .

THE SPACE BETWEEN THE WORDS

*   *   *

At first European languages did not put spaces between words:
   Igetbywithalittlehelpfrommyfriends.

About the eighth century A.D. people discovered how useful
word spaces could be:
   I get by with a little help from my friends.

This innovation is believed to have led to silent reading. "One is
tempted to compare the introduction of the space as a word
boundary to the invention of the zero in mathematics."—Roy
Harris (1986). Modern texts omit word spaces only for special
effects.

Haruki Murakami, Dance, Dance, Dance (The Sheepman)
Yourconnectionscomeundone · Yougotconfused, thinkingyou-
gotnoties. Butthere'swhereitalltiestogether · Tubersshoosnuts-
birdswhateverlittlefishandcrabsIcancatch · Wanderaround-
toomuchyou'llbebearbait · YesterdayafternoonIfoundtraces ·
Ifyouhavetowalkaroundyououghttoputabellonyourhiplikeus

James Joyce, Ulysses
Trickleaps · smackfatclacking · marqueeumbrella ·
softlyfeatured · mangongwheeltracktrolleyglarejuggernaut ·
wavenoise · wouldyousetashoe · the whowhat ·
brawlaltogether · plumeyes · brightwindbridled · sausagepink
· shorthandwriter · halffilled · mulberrycoloured

e e cummings, poems
onetwothreefourfive pigeonsjustlikethat · internalexpanding
and externalcontracting brakes Bothatonce · firstclassprivate ·
breakfastfood · talentgang · dreamslender

WARGS AND HEECHEE
Creatures and Things from Space

* * *

The names writers give to alien races and magical creatures are usually not totally alien but conform pretty well to the English spelling system or use variations on English. Despite the bizarre-looking spelling, alien names can usually be pronounced as if they were English. Compare, for example, proper names from other actual languages, such as Polish "Krzysz-pien." Given that aliens would have their own writing systems, one might ask why the English transcriptions should be so unusual in appearance!

Possible English Spellings
These use permutations of English alternative spellings.

Skrewts	Jeltz	Zang	Vatch
Noor	Ildirans	Shing	Wentals
Arisians	Rull	Synthians	Aqualish
Devaronians	Niss	Fenachrone	Poltroyans
Roog	Pigwidgin	Thralians	Heechee
Veelas	Leeminorans	Ugors	Wargs
Hydrogues	Altorians	Cardassians	

Unusual English Spellings
Often these words have Latinate plurals in "a" or "i" rather than plural "s"; clearly Latin is an influential language in outer space —indeed, the sun is often referred to as "Sol" and the inhabitants of the solar system as "Solarians."

Oankali	Ezwal	Ishi	Tok'ra
Avogwi	Arcona	Jenet	Klingons
Skandars	Ferengi	Kitonak	Ri'Dar
Verdani	Goa'uld	Animagi	Krondaku
Twi'leks	Ho'Din	Tyrenni	Klodni

| Asutra | Ondods | Wub | Xi'Dec |
| Nuri | Traeki | | |

Aliens with Impossible English Spellings
Some names use combinations of letters that do not exist in English. Alien names tend to have apostrophes, for instance, "Halyan't'a," clearly related to the dolphin name "Kjwallľk-je'koothaïllľkje'k."

Hijks	Hjorts	Kzinti	Kdatlyno
Firvulags	Tourmuj	Ghayrogs	Tnuctipun
g'Kek	Fefze	Avogwi	

HOW TO TELL A FRIENDLY ALIEN
- hostile aliens often have names with plosive sounds shown by "p/b/t/d/k/g" or "ch"—"Daleks," "Vatch," "Klingons."
- friendly aliens often have long names with plenty of "l"s and "n"s—"Alaree," "Animaloids" and "Osnomians."
- neutral aliens have names such as "Voltiscians" and "Eladeldi."
- apostrophes also seem to go with nastiness, whatever sound the apostrophe is supposed to stand for.

NOW TEST YOUR SKILLS

Aldebaranians	friend or foe?	Klodni	friend or foe?
Aleutians	friend or foe?	Krondaku	friend or foe?
Animaloids	friend or foe?	Leeminorans	friend or foe?
Arisians	friend or foe?	Lylmik	friend or foe?
Boskonians	friend or foe?	Nuri	friend or foe?
Drinats	friend or foe?	Poltroyans	friend or foe?
Eladeldi	friend or foe?	Shing	friend or foe?
Firvulags	friend or foe?	the Glotch	friend or foe?
g'Kek	friend or foe?	Tanu	friend or foe?
Hijks	friend or foe?	Triops	friend or foe?
Hjorts	friend or foe?	Velantians	friend or foe?
Kawalar	friend or foe?	Vespans	friend or foe?
Kdatlyno	friend or foe?		

Humans usually find alien names difficult to pronounce, one rechristening them "with appellations more to his liking" such as "Alice" and "Gwendolyn."

TEST

What's Wrong with Your Spelling?

*   *   *

This tests whether there are particular things wrong with your spelling. Check the right spelling for the word in the context.

1.	questionnaire	questionaire
2.	That's definate.	That's definite.
3.	supersede	supercede
4.	highly responsible	highly responsable
5.	accommodation	accomodation
6.	a complementary drink	a complimentary drink
7.	He critisized the plan.	He criticized the plan.
8.	an independent report	an independant report
9.	She refered to Bush.	She referred to Bush.
10.	open-ended categories	open-ended catagories
11.	quiet right	quite right
12.	good sense	good sence
13.	He achieved greatness.	He acheived greatness.
14.	seperate rooms	separate rooms
15.	liberal tendancy	liberal tendency
16.	ecstasy	ecstacy
17.	beginers' luck	beginner's luck
18.	sensative	sensitive
19.	They beleived the news.	They believed the news.
20.	the bare necessities	the bear necessities
21.	the percieved cost	the perceived cost
22.	the principal of gravity	the principle of gravity
23.	not necessarily true	not neccessarily true
24.	This is indispensable.	This is indispensible.
25.	It's their problem.	It's they're problem.
26.	an immence cliff	an immense cliff
27.	to conceive	to concieve
28.	cause and affect	cause and effect
29.	He recieved a postcard.	He received a postcard.
30.	reversible	reversable

Answers on page 160.

MYSTERIOUS PUBLIC NOTICES
FROM DIFFERENT COUNTRIES

* * *

INDEPENDANT STATIONARY
Two Common Mistakes

*   *   *

Two words that often give problems are "independent" and "stationery" (writing materials) versus "stationary" (motionless).

Independant Security Consultant Services Limited

Zooma Zooma Music Series
invites you to enjoy
oustanding **independant** Canadian artists
CD's $20

Independant Technologies · Gordons Independant Traders · **Independant** Libertarian Website

ULTIMATE DOLLAR & DISCOUNT STORE
$$ SOUVENIRS $$
$$ STATIONARY $$
$$ PARTY STUFF $$
$$ ELECTRONICS $$
THOUSANDS OF ITEMS $1.00 AND MORE!

With Microsoft Outlook you can set up e-mail stationary that reflects your company branding · We specialise in creating elegant custom made, hand crafted wedding invitations, Favours, and stationary for your big day · We have created some fun free stationary for your kids · Loralie provides personalized stationary invitations · Printable Stationary Online · Stationary for the Rose Lover in Everyone! · Business Accessories/Stationary · "Adhesive" means that the sticker has a sticky backing and adheres to envelopes and stationary.

UGOTTA DO IT MAGICLEIGH
Names of Racehorses

*   *   *

To name a racehorse, think of a phrase and:
- use letter names for words: Blr Diamonds R Cool, Love Me R Leave Me
- have "u" for "you": Ugotta Do It, Bustin by U
- use "k" for "c/ck" : Kreeker, Strawberry Kwik, Killarney Kutie, Finest Kreem, Kayotic
- alternate "c" and "s": Funny Cide, Sentsure, Personal Cide
- put "z" for "s/c": Tiznow, Sheza Pretty Pearl, Sarazen Bizzy Trick, Hez Not Yours, Bizzy Bee
- leave out the word spaces: Splashofscarlet, Ima Girl Judge, Paulshomemadewine, Bangbangonthedoor, Iwontell, Awholelotofmalarky, Outatime, Adreamisborn, Songinthedarkness, Double Sixisenough, Sundowncindy
- use conventional novel spellings: Brandy o' Nite, Heza Invisible Injun, A Tru Queen
- change "and" to "n": Sweet 'n Feisty, Leather N Lace, Ice n' Gold, Smashed N Splashed
- change "-ing" to "-in": Roarin Brittney, Look Whos Brakin, Sittin On a Miracle, Streakin Mufassa, Bob's Rockn'
- use "antique" spellings: Magicleigh, Lytle Creek
- imitate speech: Won More Hill
- make a pun or rhyme: Sale the Atlantic, Gneiss Limo, Untoughable, Magna Tice, A Bag of Porpourie, Reel Shiney Chrome, Shakem Elvis
- use "de"/"da" for "the," "dat" for "that": De Special Jet, Da Hoss, Dat Goose
- make spelling "mistakes": Burgandy Tower, Kaschmir, Haunted Forrest

Others

Lil E. Tee, Blurr Effort, Run Z Road, 3 Yesss, Supervelous, Gonna Do, Wwhorizontal Desire, Bagobucks, Misti Light

AN "I" FOR AN "EYE"
Matching Letters and Sounds

* * *

Here are some of the speech sounds that particular letters correspond to in English. The most common are in bold.

A **bait**, **wag**, talkative, father, many, artistically (silent)
B **bad**, doubt (silent)
C **car**, **cell**, chef, choir, chief, ocean, scissors (silent)
D **bad**, badger, watched, sandwich (silent)
E **ten**, **cedar**, be (unstressed), offer, bureau, eight, pace (silent)
F **fun**, of (only word where "f" corresponds to "v"), halfpenny (silent)
G **got**, **wage**, sabotage, gnat (silent)
H **hot**, hour (silent)
I **bit**, **bite**, legible, dirt, business (silent)
J **jam**, bijou, hallelujah
K **keen**, knife (silent)
L **left**, colonel, folk (silent)
M **time**, mnemonic (silent)
N **nice**, cling, autumn (silent)
O **phone**, **dog**, door, book, word, youth, cow, tough, boy
P **pot**, elephant, psychology (silent)
Q **baroque**
R **bread**, third
S **see**, **dies**, sugar, illusion, island (silent)
T **stop**, **them**, **theory**, catch, nation, equation, buffet (silent)
U **but**, **fruit**, burn, use, full, guest (silent)
V **live**, leitmotiv
W **wind**, who, write (silent)
X **sex**, Xena, exist
Y **yes**, martyr, ratify, funny
Z **zoo**, waltz, rendezvous (silent)

'ARF A MO GUV
London Accent Spelling in Novels

* * *

British novelists have shown London speech through spelling, from the Cockney of older days to the modern "Estuary English" called after the Thames estuary area, where it is spoken. Many of the features represent what everybody actually says, "wot" for "what," or nonstandard accents, " 'arry" for "Harry"—h dropping happens in many British accents.

Charles Dickens, 1836

"Well . . . the adwantage o' the plan's hobvious."

"That's the pint, sir . . . out vuth it, as the father said to the child, wen he swallowed a farden."

George Bernard Shaw, 1916

"Cheer ap, Keptin; n' baw ya flahr orf a pore gel."

"Waw not, gavner? Ahrs is a Free Tride nition."

Michael Moorcock, 1976

"I still fink 'e shouldn'ta moved me wivvout arskin'."

"Nar! It woz nuffink forin. . . . Darn the 'atch, then."

"Cor! Wot a scorcher! . . . D'yer like it? I 'ad it run up special for yer corernation. Lovely turnart, innit?"

Iain Banks, Brixton, 2003

"Wot sort of party was this you was boaf at, anyway?"

"Bit of a accent though, asn't he? Dontya fink?"

". . . that's in everybody's inarest so that the money keeps comin slidin froo."

Eye dialect features (nonstandard spelling of standard everyday pronunciations)

wot, wen, woz, useter, wenever, pore, 'till, yer, cos

Features that are part of many nonstandard British accents

"h" dropping on nouns and verbs: 'appening, 'atch

"in" for "ing": arskin', comin

Features possibly specific to London area

"f" or "v" for "th": nuffink, fink, somefink, smoov, boaf, froo

extra "h"s: hobvious, Hinglishmen, hinfluence

vowel sounds: ahses (houses), darn (down), ap (up), git (get)

SHEAR DELIGHT IN HAIR DOOZ
Hairdressers' Salons

* * *

Los Angeles
A Kut Above	Hair Is Us	U-Next
Cut'n Up	Haircut Express	2 Gether
Hair Dooz	Pooh Da Tightest	Hair Mechanix
The Hair'em	Hairllucination	Hairloom
Hair II Hair	Shear Delight	

Cardiff, Wales
Simon Sez	Essensuals	Head 2 Toe
Curls 2 Hair	Kutz Hair Design	Blew Room
Hair F X	Hairazors	

Jamaica
Kris Kut	Aestheque	Klippers
Klassique	Hair 'N' You	Klymax

Glasgow, Scotland
Crazy Cutz	Ellgeez	Blew Hair Studio
Streaks Ahead	Cut and Dried	Cut-n-Crew

Melbourne, Australia
Bamboozal Salon	Ambyanz Fyshwick	Hiz & Herz
Hairific	Clip'N'Shave	Hairrroom
Short Black 'N' Sides	E-Clipz	Headmasters
	Headworx	

Singapore
Hairaway 'N' Unisex	Nulook	Hawaii Five-0 (His)
	X'treme De Beaute	Hair Cut Inn

Houston
Fazes Hair Studio	Ken's Kutting Shoppe	Oassis Hair Salon
Hair After		Salon F X
Mane Street	Le Nails Et Beaute	Xute Looks Cuts

EARLY AMERICAN
ALPHABET BOOKS

*   *   *

1750 *The Story of an Apple Pye*	1796	*Some alternatives, (from different early sources)*
A Apple-Pye	A Apple	A was an angler.
B bit it.	B Bull	B was a blind-man.
C cut it.	C Cat	C was a cutpurse.
D divided it.	D Dog	D was a drunkard.
E eat it.	E Egg	E was an esquire.
F faught for it.	F Fish	F was a farmer.
G got it.	G Goat	G was a gamester.
H had it.	H Hog	H was a hunter.
I inspected it.	I —	I was an innkeeper.
J join'd for it.	J Judge	J was a joiner.
K kept it.	K King	K was King William.
L long'd for it.	L Lion	L was a lady.
M mourned for it.	M Mouse	M was a miser.
N nodded at it.	N Nag	N was a nobleman.
O open'd it.	O Owl	O was an oyster girl.
P peep'd in't.	P Peacock	P was a parson.
Q quarter'd it.	Q Queen	Q was a Quaker.
R ran for't.	R Robin	R was a robber.
S snatch'd it.	S Squirrel	S was a sailor.
T turned it.	T Top	T was a tinker.
U —	U —	U was a usurer.
V view'd it.	V Vine	V was a vintner.
W won it.	W Whale	W was a watchman.
XYZ &.	X Xerxes	X was expensive.
I wish I had a	Y Young Lamb	Y was a yokel.
Piece of it now	Z Zany	Z was a zebra.
in my Hand.		

ANNUITY/DUITY
American Rhymes

*   *   *

The many alternatives within English spelling and the large number of homophones make possible a vast number of rhymes, usually for comic effect.

Ogden Nash
foemen / abdomen · Sahara / narra (narrow) · eerier / posteerier · mariner / barrener · parsley / gharsley · annuity / duity · talcum / walcum · household / mouseholed

Don Marquis
Methooslum / oozly-goozlum · worter / hadn't orter · hippopotamusses / octopusses · gobble 'em / problem · gorillars / armadillers · facks / axe · beard / skeered

Tom Lehrer
Hahvard / discahvered · in the war / esprit de corps · the guy who's got religion'll / Tell you if your sin's original · abdomen / Roman · could have her / her sister's cadaver · murdah / *Das Lied von der Erde* · Oedipus / duck-billed platypus · Alma / embalma · relations, sparing no expense, 'll / Send some useless old utensil · sturgeons / detergeons · quickenin' / strych'nine · quibbled / ribald · a funeral / sooner or'l (later)

Lorenz Hart
sad / Noel Ca-ad (Coward) · oven / love an' · Turkey / Albuquerque · Open Sesame / less o' me · antelope / cantaloupe · Niag'ra / aggra- (vate) · angel / change'll · Dietrich / sweet trick · nonce / pense

BAD DOGZ IN DA HOOD
Drum 'n' Bass

*   *   *

Ya ya ya

What Ya gonna do?	Ja know ya	Ya Rockin'

Da da da

Da Intalex	Da base II dark	In da Hood
Rrroll da beat	Turn da lites down	From da east

"z" for "s"

Bad Dogz	Metalheadz	Homeboyz
Clear Skyz	Dope Skillz	Elementz of Noize
Saturnz Return	Vibez	Junglizm
Kartoonz	Hard Noize	Fuze

"k" for "c/ch"

Tekniq	Jaz Klash	New Skool
Konkrete	Jungle Kosmos	Kram

"a/az" for "er/ers" (with variants)

Flava's	Bounty Killaz	Masta Ace
Dreama	True Playaz	Gangsta Prizna
Original Nuttah	Soul Beat Runna	

Others

Back 2 Life	Ganja Kru	Rugged N Raw
Beat Dis	Geese Toon	Scribes 'N' Dusty
Blows T' the Nose	Glok Track	Shy FX
Boomin' Back Atcha	Images/Dezires	Skratchadelikizm
Brockin' Out	J. Walkin'	Slip Thru
Check the Teq	Jon E-2 Bad	Smokin' Cans
Cool Rok Stuff	Lo Life	Street Tuff
Dark Crystl	Majistrate	Suecide
DJ Trax	Manix	Swan-E
Dred Bass	Mo' wax	Triffic Tunes
The Eff word	Nu Energy	Trip II the Moon
Ellis Dee	Phuture	We are E
E-Nuff	Punk-Roc	Who runs 'Tings?
Firin' Line	Rinsin' Lyrics	
	Ruffneck ragga	

RULES FOR SILENT "E"

*   *   *

THE LETTER "E" IS SILENT:

- to show a vowel is "long" (free), not "short" (checked)

rate	rat	Pete	pet	cute	cut
ripe	rip	code	cod		

- to distinguish surnames from nouns (see p. 2)

Cooke	cook	Howe	how	Paine	pain
Moore	moor	Goode	good	Crewe	crew

- to obey the Three Letter Rule (p. 10) by indicating "content" words rather than "structure" words such as prepositions

bye	by	ore	or	inn	in

- to prevent "v" and "u" occurring on their own at the ends of words, perhaps because these were the same letter up to the middle of the seventeenth century
  "v": have, love, glove, dove, live; except for: spiv, rev, lav
  "u": glue, plague, continue, due

- to show that words are not plural

please	pleas	moose	moos	tense	tens

- to distinguish different consonant sounds

bathe	bath	breathe	breath	halve	half

- to distinguish written words with the same pronunciation

belle	bell	fiancée	fiancé	borne	born
pie	pi	browse	brows	lapse	laps

- after double consonants in some words originally from French

cassette	usherette	baguette
gaffe	rosette	cigarette

- after final consonant plus "l"

bubble	middle	treacle

SCORES ON A DIFFICULT WORDS SPELLING TEST

* * *

An online test of English spelling looked at how well people did on twenty difficult words. Here are how many people out of a hundred spelled each word correctly.

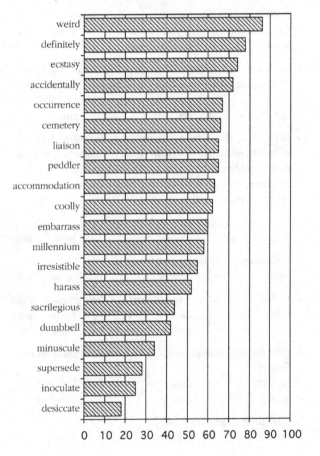

DANGER: SPELLING CHEQUER AT WORK

* * *

A Newsletter (Anon)
They're know miss steaks in this newsletter cause we used special soft wear witch checks yore spelling. It is mower or lass a weigh too verify. How ever is can knot correct arrows inn punctuation ore usage: an it will not fined words witch are miss used butt spelled rite. Four example; a paragraph could have mini flaws but wood bee past by the spell checker. And it wont catch the sentence fragment which you. Their fore, the massage is that proofreading is knot eliminated, it is still berry muck reek wired.

Guess the correct form of these names supplied by a spelling checker
Pop musicians: Wring Tsar, Shirley Basest, Frank Signature, Joan Baize, Mick Jaguar, Justin Timberline, Dolly Partook, Tammy Wined, Ammonium, Frank Sappier
Politicians: Colin Power, Nelson Manuela, George Shirk, Dick Teeny, Eva Peon, Hugo Chivvies, Fiddler Castor
Film stars: George Cloned, Gwynneth Poltroon, Mewl Gibson, Winnow Ryder, Johnny Dew, Walter Mother, Buster Beaton, Henry Fondue, Nicole Camden, Russell Crone, Michael Canine, Brad Pity, Lauren Banal, Merely Stern
Shakespearean characters: Prospers, Aphelia, Titanic, Fester, Laureates, Madcap, Bantu, Hearty, Orisons, Ethel, Ago
Sports people: Andorra Ages, Michael Schemata, David Buckram, Paella, Sterner Williams, Bong, Mark Spots, Martina Whinges, Diego Meridian

The only ones not immediately obvious are perhaps: Ammonium (Eminem), Bong (Borg), Laureates (Laertes), Madcap (MacDuff), Bantu (Banquo), Hearty (Horatio), Orisons (Orsino), Ethel (Othello).

FLEA EZE AND VIOXX
Spellings of Drugs

*   *   *

Take it easy with:

Sugar-Eze	Flea Eze	Skin-Eze
Blisteze	Chest-Eze	Diareze
Digesta-eze	Arthri-Eze	Breathe-Eze
Herp-Eze	Pollon-Eze	Snore-Eze
Ear-Eze	Sooth-Eze	Progesta-Eze
Breathe-Eze	Rest-Eze	Sting-Eze

Names with "z," "x" or "q": according to some branding experts, these letters convey a sense of dynamism and the future.

Zyrtec	Xalatan	Pneumovax
Xenical	Zithromax	Je-Vax
Aropax	Uvadex	Xylocaine
Xanax	Zovirax	Zocor
Mykrox	Xylometazoline	Imitrex
Prozac	Zyvox	
Xylapan	Aludrox	

Final "-one"/"-ine," etc.

Claritin	Ceftin	Absorbine
Tetracycline	Vumon	Prednisone
Sulfamylon	Thorazine	Ritalin

Double vowels and consonants

Aggrenox	Vioxx	Lexxel
Hyzaar	Neggram	Quaalude

"y" rather than "i"

Go-Lytely	Aci-Je	Bendryl
Wygesic	Robinul	Amytal
Pedialyte	Gynazole	Flagyl
Lufyllin	Florinef	Dyphylline
Gastrolyte	Allerdryl	Cycrin
Nydrazid	Dynabac	Zyban

Unpronounceable names

Ulr-La	CeeNU	Ddva

FUJI APPLES AND ARUGULA
Spelling in Cookery

* * *

Cookery terms now include many words that break the usual spelling patterns of English, although they do not necessarily follow the spelling in the languages they came from.

IDENTIFY THE LANGUAGE *Answers on page 162.*

1. broccoli	8. chili	14. mangosteen
2. mangetout	9. shiitake	15. kumquats
3. bok choi	mushrooms	16. kiwifruit
4. okra	10. guava	17. medjol dates
5. zucchini	11. primavera salad	18. fuji apples
6. lollo rosso	12. coleslaw	19. pistachios
7. avocado	13. papaya	20. satsumas

The spelling of food on menus
Cajun: gumbo, jambalaya, po-boy, etouffee
Italian: bruschetta, carpaccio, polenta, prosciutto, penne, linguine, zucchini, osso buco, risotto, tiramisu, pizza
French: jus, beignets, confit, ratatouille, mesclun
Polish: kielbasy, bigos, blintz
Greek: baklava, moussaka, souvlaki, tsatziki, taramasalata
Chinese: chow mein, wonton, congee
Thai: satay, Tom Yum, pad Thair
Indian: samosa, pakora, bhaji, papadam, Gobhi, tikka, biryani
Spanish: ceviche, ensalada, paella, chorizo
Japanese: sushi, miso, tofu, tempura, sashimi, ramen
Mexican: nachos, chili con carne, quesadillas, tamales, tortillas, fajitas, burrito, tacos
German: schnitzel, knackwurst, sauerbraten
Moroccan: cous cous, kefta, hummus, falafel, tabouli

STOCKBROCKING EMPORIAM
Newspaper Mistakes

* * *

These mistakes come from printed sources such as newspapers and phone books. Some of the advertisements appeared like this week after week.

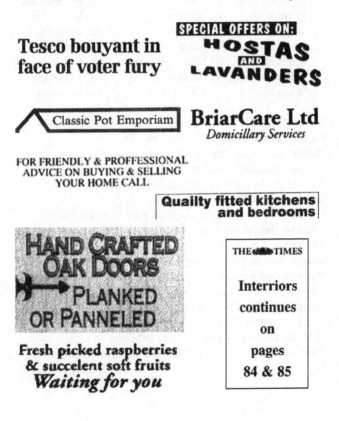

Independent Stockbrocking Service

Tesco bouyant in face of voter fury

SPECIAL OFFERS ON:
HOSTAS AND **LAVANDERS**

Classic Pot Emporiam

BriarCare Ltd
Domicillary Services

FOR FRIENDLY & PROFFESSIONAL
ADVICE ON BUYING & SELLING
YOUR HOME CALL

**Quailty fitted kitchens
and bedrooms**

HAND CRAFTED
OAK DOORS
→ PLANKED
OR PANNELED

THE TIMES

Interriors
continues
on
pages
84 & 85

Fresh picked raspberries
& succelent soft fruits
Waiting for you

NO WAY SIS AND FONEY M
Cover Bands

*   *   *

The names of cover bands need to suggest the originals while making it clear
they are not the real thing through their
spelling, puns, etc.

Abba: Abba Solutely, Abbasolutely Live, Abbalanche, Rebjorn,
Björn Again, FABBA

The Beatles: The Beatalls, The Beatels, The Beetles UK, The
Fantaztic Fore, Beatnix, Beatals, Zeatles

The Rolling Stones: The Rolling Clones, The Rollin' Tones, The
Strolling Bones

UB40: UB4T, We Be 40

Pink Floyd: Floydian Slip, Pink Fraud, Think Freud

The Who: Who's Who, The Guess Who, The Wholigans

Oasis: Oasisnt, No Way Sis, Okasis

Match the cover artists with their originals:

1.	Robbing Williams	Hear'say
2.	Cheeky Monkees	Eminem
3.	Ceilidh Minogue	Queen
4.	Alanis Moreorless	AC/DC
5.	Lets' Eppelin	Black Sabbath
6.	Guns N Poses	Robbie Williams
7.	M & N	Nirvana
8.	Near Say	T-Rex
9.	Nearvana	Tom Jones
10.	Qween	Stereophonics
11.	T-Rextasy	The Monkees
12.	AC/Seedy	Guns N' Roses
13.	Clone Roses	Led Zeppelin
14.	Stereophonies	Stone Roses
15.	A-Tom-ic Jones	Kylie Minogue
16.	Slack Babbath	Alanis Morissette

FRYERISH POKER MOM
Joke Spellings in Sitcom Episode Names

* * *

Futurama episodes
A Fishful of Dollars

A Head in the Polls

A Bicyclops Built for Two

Jurassic Bark

The Route of All Evil

Obsoletely Fabulous

I Second That Emotion

The Cryonic Woman

Parasites Lost

The Luck of the Fryrish

Roswell That Ends Well

Where the Buggalo Roam

Frasier
Flour Child

Chess Pains

Star Mitzvah

Guns N' Neuroses

How to Bury a Millionaire

A Tsar Is Born

It Takes Two to Tangle

War of the Words

Frasier Has Spokane

Bristle While You Work

No Sex Please, We're Skittish

The Simpsons
The Crepes of Wrath

Krusty Gets Kancelled

Much Apu About Nothing

The Canine Mutiny

The Joy of Sect

D'oh-in' in the Wind

Monty Can't Buy Me Love

Grift of the Magi

Pokey Mom

Children of a Lesser Clod

My Big Fat Geek Wedding

The *Fawlty Towers* Hotel Sign
FARTY TOWER	WARTY TOWELS	FAW TY TO WER
WATERY FOWLS	FAWLTY TOWERS	FATTY OWLS
FAWLTY TOWER	FLAY OTTERS	FLOWERY TWATS
FARTY TOWELS		

KUTE THINGS FOR KIDS

* * *

Novel spelling for children's products uses a blend of old-style business-name spellings—"Kandoo"—and informal spoken forms—"Rollin' Rumblin' Dump."

Toys

Jettmobile
Jump-o-lene
Happitime Farm Set
Konvertible Kite
Bratz dolls
Clatterpillar
Cubo
Rompa
Roobix Cube

Press 'n Play Lights Ball
Kommunication Kidz
Play Doh Fun Factory
Little Tikes Rockin' Puppy
Koosh Critters
Draw n Giggle Barney
Hip-O-Boat
Rollin' Rumblin' Dump

Feeding, Drinking and Sanitation

Easiflow Beaker
Pampers Kandoo wipes
Kooshies ultra reusable nappy
Just Pooh potty
Slo-go aeroplane exerciser
Cuddle 'n' dry robe
Flo-Control bottles

Tommee Tippee Potette
Comfi trainer seat
Pampers Kandoo
Babytec bottle
Nappysaurus Fleece Wrap
Playskool

Furniture, Etc.

Whoozit Photo Album
Eggsercizer Lil' Wheels

Supa Squashy Sofa
Jumbo Skwish

Transport

Kiddiwalker
Metrolite travel system
Duolite twin pushchair
Urban Detour Xtreme

Li'l Lady Buggy
Britax Practical
Swift Lite Buggy
Chicco Xplorer

DUN LAOGHAIRE SIOUXIE
Spelling Humor

*   *   *

Dun Laoghaire (Dun Laoghaire [near Dublin] is said "done leery")
There was a young man from Dun Laoghaire
Who propounded an interesting thaoghaire:
That the language of Erse
Has a shortage of verse
'Cos the spelling makes poets so waoghaire.

Potato
If GH stands for P as in Hiccough
If OUGH stands for O as in Dough
If PHTH stands for T as in Phthisis
If EIGH stands for A as in Neighbour
If TTE stands for T as in Gazette
If EAU stands for O as in Plateau
The right way to spell
POTATO should be GHOUGHPHTHEIGHTTEEAU!

Ambrose Bierce, The Devil's Dictionary
A spelling reformer indicted
For fudge was before the court cicted.
The judge said: "Enough—
His candle we'll snough,
And his sepulchre shall not be whicted."

Charles Follen Adams, An Orthographic Lament
If an S and an I and an O and a U
With an X at the end spell Su;
And an E and a Y and an E spell I,
Pray what is a speller to do?
Then, if also an S and an I and a G
And an HED spell side,
There's nothing much left for a speller to do
But to go commit siouxeyesighed

The **original** **1623**	To be, or not to be, that is the Queſtion : Whether 'tis Nobler in the minde to ſuffer The Slings and Arrowes of outragious Fortune, Or to take Armes againſt a Sea of troubles, And by oppoſing end them.
The IPA **Hamlet** **p. 52**	Hamlet: /tə bi ɔɹ nɒ tə bi ðæt ɪz ðə kwɛstʃən wɛðəɹ tɪz nobləɹ ɪn ðə main tə sʌfəɹ ðə slɪŋz ən æɹoʊz əv aʊtɹeɪdʒəz fɔɹtʃun ən baɪ əpoʊzɪn ɛn ðəm/.
Th txt **msg Hmlt** **p. 47**	2 b or not 2 b, that s th question: wetha tis nobla in th mind 2 suffa th slings n arros of outragus 4tune, or 2 take arms against a c of trublz, n by opposin end thm.
The Cut **Spelng** **Hamlet** **p. 100**	To be, or not to be, that is th question: Wethr tis noblr in th mind to sufr Th slings and aros of outrajus fortune, Or to take arms against a se of trubls, And by oposing end them.
The Badly **Spelt** **Hamlet**	Too bee or not too bee, that is the question: Weather tis nobbler in the mind too suffer The slings and arrows of outragous foretune Or too take arms against a see of trubbles And buy oposing end them.
The **Homophonic** **Hamlet** **p. 40**	Two bee, awe knot two bee, that is the question: Weather 'tis know blur inn the mined two suffer The slings and arose of out ragers four tune, Awe two take alms against a see of troubles, And buy a posing end them.

COMPETETIVE AND GURANTEED
Mistakes on Painted Signs

* * *

Competetive Rates of Commision

ELROND AND BOMBUR
Tolkien's Names

*   *   *

In the Middle Earth created by J. R. R. Tolkien in *The Lord of the Rings*, the *Silmarillion, Unfinished Tales*, etc., the characters come from several races that speak different languages, chiefly indicated by the spelling. Sort these out into the relevant languages. Warning: these come from the books, not necessarily the films.

		Elves	Humans	Dwarves	Hobbits	Maiar	Others
1.	Balin						
2.	Galadriel						
3.	Eowen						
4.	Gimli						
5.	Aragorn						
6.	Gandalf						
7.	Arwen						
8.	Bombur						
9.	Saruman						
10.	Bilbo						
11.	Celeborn						
12.	Meriadioc						
13.	Fangorn						
14.	Legolas						
15.	Telchar						
16.	Beren						
17.	Frodo						
18.	Sauron						
19.	Theoden						
20.	Glorfindel						
21.	Beleg						

Answers on page 162.

Maiar: the first beings, the Ainur, consisting of Valar and Maiar
Elves: First Born race, immortal

Humans: Second Born race, mortal
Dwarves: race created in secret to be strong and unyielding
Hobbits: the Halflings (three and a half feet tall)
Ents: the tree-folk

TEST
Odd Word Out

*   *   *

One of the words in each of these lists has a different sound correspondence for the letters than the others, at least in a General American accent.

1.	**ch**	chicken	cheese	chef
2.	**ei**	weigh	ceiling	receive
3.	**x**	Xena	X-ray	xylophone
4.	**gh**	though	ought	gherkin
5.	**ow**	cow	show	now
6.	**c**	cent	call	Cuthbert
7.	**s**	ask	bids	scan
8.	**l**	bill	almond	almoner
9.	**e**	ego	egg	bed
10.	**m**	mnemonic	autumn	lemming
11.	**th**	this	then	thin
12.	**oa**	abroad	goat	load
13.	**a**	father	chalk	Brahms
14.	**oo**	food	book	brood
15.	**ph**	physics	Ralph	shepherd
16.	**y**	city	youth	you
17.	**au**	sausage	bauble	saucer
18.	**wh**	whole	whale	while
19.	**o**	above	aroma	cover
20.	**p**	corps	corpse	copse
21.	**u**	bun	but	brute
22.	**ae**	eon	aerial	anemia
23.	**h**	house	honest	hour
24.	**cc**	accept	succeed	broccoli
25.	**gu**	tongue	disguise	guard

Answers on page 163.

MODERN TYPEFACES
FOR ENGLISH

*   *   *

The use of typefaces is a vital part of the modern English writing system, now that they are under the control of most writers. Fonts like Times New Roman, with cross-strokes (serifs) and varying line widths, are thought better for continuous text such as books. Fonts like Gill Sans and Verdana, without cross-strokes (sans serif) and with even width, are better for display and short pieces of text. Mistral tends to be used in posters.

Times New Roman *(serif, Stanley Morison, 1932)*
abcdefghijklmnopqrstuvwxyz?!&
ABCDEFGHIJKLMNOPQRSTUVWXYZ
The great enemy of clear language is insincerity.
Designed for *The Times* newspaper, derived from Plantin and classical Roman letters.

Verdana *(sans serif, Matthew Carter, 1996)*
abcdefghijklmnopqrstuvwxyz?!&
ABCDEFGHIJKLMNOPQRSTUVWXYZ
The great enemy of clear language is insincerity.
Designed to be legible on monitor screens and massively used in Web pages.

Gill Sans *(sans serif, Eric Gill, 1928)*
abcdefghijklmnopqrstuvwxyz?!&
ABCDEFGHIJKLMNOPQRSTUVWXYZ
The great enemy of clear language is insincerity.
Linked to Edward Johnston's font for the London Underground (1916), an adapted form of which (New Johnston) is still in use.

Mistral (joined-up brush strokes, Roger Excoffon, 1953)
abcdefghijklmnopqrstuvwxyz?!&
ABCDEFGHIJKLMNOPQRSTUVWXYZ
The great enemy of clear language is insincerity.
Perhaps the first to achieve an apparently joined-up effect.

A PAGE FOR U

* * *

TEST
American Versus British Style Around the World
* * *

The spelling of English varies in different countries according to how much they favor British or American styles of spelling for particular words. Which of these newspaper examples seem more American style, which more British style?

1. *Ghana:* December 2004 would be the first time that a civilian government . . . is going to fulfil a full term.
2. *Israel:* Channel 2 does viewers a favor by offering a 23:05 rescreening of *Monsoon*.
3. *Lebanon:* Dubai has more than 600 jewelry shops, the densest concentration in the world.
4. *Russia:* The dialogue with Moscow, which is lately gaining momentum, is highly appreciated in Georgia.
5. *Canada:* The alliance will continue to plow ahead on its own.
6. *China:* Richard Pearson, an independent Canadian archeologist . . .
7. *Australia:* A Briton has been jailed for 15 years in Vietnam for murdering his travelling companion . . .
8. *Borneo:* Two unemployed local men pleaded guilty yesterday to stealing 29 kg of used aluminium.

Labor (American)/Labour (British) Around the World
Korea: escalating labor unrest
Canada: the restructuring would have to work around labour laws.
Israel: High-tech labor demand down 40% in 2003
Thailand: The senior government official who fell to his death out of the Labour Ministry . . .
New Zealand: Handcuffed labour criticised
India: . . . labour commissioner MB Gajre . . .
Singapore: Left-wing Labor MPs
Bangladesh: child-labour education programme
Czech Republic: the labor rights situation
Nigeria: the Nigeria Labour Congress (NLC)
Answers on page 163.

SAMUEL JOHNSON
Preface to A Dictionary of the English Language *1755*

*　*　*

I found it necessary to distinguish those irregularities that are
inherent in our tongue, and perhaps coeval with it, from others
which the ignorance or negligence of later writers has produced. Every language has its anomalies, which, though incon-
venient, and in themselves once unnecessary, must be tolerated
among the imperfections of human things, and which require
only to be registered, that they may not be increased, and ascer-
tained, that they may not be confounded: but every language
has likewise its improprieties and absurdities, which it is the
duty of the lexicographer to correct or proscribe.

As language was at its beginning merely oral, all words of
necessary or common use were spoken before they were written; and while they were unfixed by any visible signs, must
have been spoken with great diversity, as we now observe those
who cannot read catch sounds imperfectly, and utter them neg-
ligently. When this wild and barbarous jargon was first reduced
to an alphabet, every penman endeavoured to express, as he
could, the sounds which he was accustomed to pronounce or to
receive, and vitiated in writing such words as were already
vitiated in speech. The powers of the letters, when they were
applied to a new language, must have been vague and
unsettled, and therefore different hands would exhibit the
same sound by different combinations.

From this uncertain pronunciation arise in a great part the
various dialects of the same country, which will always be
observed to grow fewer, and less different, as books are
multiplied; and from this arbitrary representation of sounds
by letters, proceeds that diversity of spelling observable in
the Saxon remains, and I suppose in the first books of every
nation, . . .

THE FREQUENCY OF LETTERS
IN AMERICAN ENGLISH

* * *

The letters of a language do not occur with the same frequency. The figures here are calculated from Mark Twain's *Huckleberry Finn* (109,000 words; 433,000 characters). The most frequent letter is "e" with 46,661 (10.8%), the least frequent is "q" with 173 (0.01%).

LETTER FREQUENCIES FOR ENGLISH

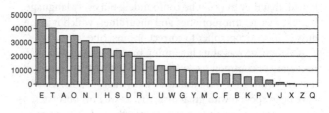

DIGRAPH FREQUENCIES

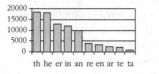

TRIGRAPH FREQUENCIES

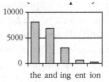

Such information helps code breakers to find out which language is concealed in a message and to work out which letters have been substituted for which, as described in Edgar Allan Poe's "The Gold Bug." Helen Gaines's *Cryptanalysis* gives the high frequency group as "e t a o n i r s h," the top ten digraphs as "th in er re an he ar en ti te," and the top five trigraphs as "the ing and ion ent," slightly different from those here.

OUTLAWZ AND CUTE CAIT
British and American Novel Spellings

* * *

The British and American editions of this book revealed differences over how novel spelling are handled in American and British English. Can you tell which are which?

Pop Groups (see p. 22)

Gorillaz	Am ☐	Brit ☐	Puddle of		
6 Teens	Am ☐	Brit ☐	Mudd	Am ☐	Brit ☐
Eminem	Am ☐	Brit ☐	4-Hero	Am ☐	Brit ☐
Nuckledz	Am ☐	Brit ☐	Outlawz	Am ☐	Brit ☐
			Black II Basics	Am ☐	Brit ☐

Show Dogs (see p. 32)

Knot-A-Yacht	Am ☐	Brit ☐	Mistymoor	Am ☐	Brit ☐
Miss B'Havin	Am ☐	Brit ☐	Up N'Adam	Am ☐	Brit ☐
For-U-To-N-V	Am ☐	Brit ☐	Justine Thyme	Am ☐	Brit ☐
Brite As A			Nice Tri	Am ☐	Brit ☐
Button	Am ☐	Brit ☐			

License Plates (see p. 38)

2FAST4U	Am ☐	Brit ☐	G1 RLY	Am ☐	Brit ☐
UNC 1E	Am ☐	Brit ☐	CYCOPTH	Am ☐	Brit ☐
CHZHED	Am ☐	Brit ☐	81TCH	Am ☐	Brit ☐
S4 NDY	Am ☐	Brit ☐	P9 YCO	Am ☐	Brit ☐

Racehorses (see p. 114)

Funny Cide	Am ☐	Brit ☐	Hez Not Yours	Am ☐	Brit ☐
Luvah Girl	Am ☐	Brit ☐	Nothin' Leica		
Cute Cait	Am ☐	Brit ☐	Dane	Am ☐	Brit ☐
Iwontell	Am ☐	Brit ☐	Outatime	Am ☐	Brit ☐
			Scooby Who	Am ☐	Brit ☐

Hairdressers (see p. 117)

Mane Street	Am ☐	Brit ☐	Hair Dooz	Am ☐	Brit ☐
Oassis Salon	Am ☐	Brit ☐	Curl Up 'N' Dye	Am ☐	Brit ☐
Split Enz	Am ☐	Brit ☐	Stylelistiks	Am ☐	Brit ☐

Song Titles (see p. 147)

Bangin' Man	Am ☐	Brit ☐	You boyz	Am ☐	Brit ☐
Emale	Am ☐	Brit ☐	make big		
Myzterious	Am ☐	Brit ☐	noize		
Mizster Jones	Am ☐	Brit ☐	Bagg Up	☐Am	☐Brit

Answers on page 164.

MILLENIUM EXSTACY
Spelling Mistakes on the Web

*   *   *

The percentage of incorrect spellings on Web pages compared to the correct spelling. Sometimes the incorrect spelling may be correct in another language and may distort the figures.

minuscule	(miniscule: labeled as "erroneous" in *OED*; as variant in *Webster's*)	42%
millennium	(millenium, milenium, milennium)	32.7
supersede	(supercede, superceed)	26.1
accommodation	(accomodation, acommodation)	19.7
irresistible	(irresistable)	13.7
ecstasy	(exstacy, ecstacy)	13.5
embarrass	(embaras, embarass)	12.2
desiccate	(desicate, dessicate, dessiccate)	10.6
definitely	(definately, difinately)	10.4
pronunciation	(pronounciation)	10.2
separate	(seperate)	9.7
necessary	(neccesary, necesary, neccesary)	9.1
broccoli	(brocolli, brocoli—alternative in *Webster's*)	7.1
address	(adress, adres)	6.5
cemetery	(cemetary, semetary, but Stephen King book *Pet Sematary*)	6.3
occurrence	(occurence, ocurence)	6.1
independent	(independant)	5.7
questionnaire	(questionaire)	4.8
liaison	(liaision)	4.7
useful	(usefull)	4.3
referring	(refering)	3.1
recommend	(recomend, reccomend, reccommend)	3.1
liaison	(liason)	2.7
parallel	(paralel, parallell, paralell, parralel)	2.3
receive	(recieve)	1.8
beginning	(begining)	1.6
paid	(payed)	0.7

GREENGROCER'S ON THE STREET

* * *

Nouns with plural "s" in English do not have an apostrophe; that is to say, the plural form is "books" not "book's"; "teams," not "team's." However, street notices, shop labels and advertisements frequently advertise "melon's," "cauliflower's" and "carrot's"—hence this is often called the greengrocer's apostrophe.

*   *   *

I come now to another part of your letter, which is the orthography, if I may call bad spelling ORTHOGRAPHY. You spell induce, ENDUCE; and grandeur, you spell grandURE; two faults of which few of my housemaids would have been guilty. I must tell you that orthography, in the true sense of the word, is so absolutely necessary for a man of letters; or a gentleman, that one false spelling may fix ridicule upon him for the rest of his life; and I know a man of quality, who never recovered the ridicule of having spelled WHOLESOME without the w.

Reading with care will secure everybody from false spelling; for books are always well spelled, according to the orthography of the times. Some words are indeed doubtful, being spelled differently by different authors of equal authority; but those are few; and in those cases every man has his option, because he may plead his authority either way; but where there is but one right way, as in the two words above mentioned, it is unpardonable and ridiculous for a gentleman to miss it; even a woman of a tolerable education would despise and laugh, at a lover, who should send her an ill-spelled billet-doux. I fear and suspect, that you have taken it into your head, in most cases, that the matter is all, and the manner little or nothing. If you have, undeceive yourself, and be convinced that, in everything, the manner is full as important as the matter. If you speak the sense of an angel, in bad words and with a disagreeable utterance, nobody will hear you twice, who can help it. If you write epistles as well as Cicero, but in a very bad hand, and very ill-spelled, whoever receives will laugh at them; and if you had the figure of Adonis, with an awkward air and motions, it will disgust instead of pleasing. Study manner, therefore, in everything, if you would be anything.

SPELLINGS 'R' US

* * *

Elephants R Us	Fantasy Sports R Us
Babies R Us	Ratz R Us
the NIH Molecules R Us	Owls "R" US
Utility	Cowhides R Us
Bricks 'R Us	Cells R Us
Bannerz R US	Squirrels R Us
Disabilities-R-Us	Aliens R' Us!
Bald R Us	Chats-R-Us
Danes-R-Us	Grants R' Us,
asian-brides-r-us.com	Cats R Us
Goats R Us	Vans-R-Us
Amish-r-us.com	Casinos R Us

Extensions from the pattern
The-Web-is-us.com
bikesrnottoys.com
Perfumeisus.com
Chartsisus.com
Hair Is Us
golfisus.net

STREETZ 4 U AND EYE:
SONG TITLES

*   *   *

The spelling of song titles often deliberately shows the singer's accent.

Songs Performed by Prince

If Eye Was the Man in Ur Life	Strollin'
What Do U Want Me 2 Do	Sensual everafter
Lovesexy	Damn U
I Would Die 4 U	Live 4 love
U Got the Look	Emale
Gett Off	Old friends 4 sale
Money Don't Matter 2 Night	Love 2 the 9s
Take Me with U	Anna Stesia
Anotherloverholenyohead	

Linton Kwesi Johnson (Jamaica and London)

All Wi Don Is Defendin	If I Waz a Tap Natch Poet
Di Great Insohreckshan	Independent intavenshan
Dirty langwidge dub	It noh funny
Doun Di Road	Liesense Fi Kill
Dubbin Di Revalueshan	Sense Outta Nansense
Fite dem back	Tings an' Times
Forces of vicktry	Wat about di workin' claas?

Chingy

Right Thurr	Holidae In
He's Herre	Sample Dat Ass
Wurrs My Cash	Mobb Wit Me
Bagg Up	

2PAC

The Streetz R Deathrow

Heartz of Men

Ballad of a Dead Soulja

Letter 2 My Unborn

Ambitionz Az a Ridah

I Ain't Mad at Cha

Never B Peace

Heaven Ain't Hard 2 Find

Last Wordz

What'z Ya Phone No.

2Pacalypse

Now Keep Ya Head Up

2 of Amerikaz Most Wanted

How Do U Want It

ANSWERS

* * *

DIFFICULT WORDS SPELLING TEST

(p. 4)

1. dessicate — **desiccate** *(circled)* — desicate
2. **ecstasy** *(circled)* — exstacy — ecstasy
3. milenium — millenium — **millennium** *(circled)*
4. dumbel — **dumbbell** *(circled)* — dumbell
5. seperate — **separate** *(circled)* — seperete
6. necesary — neccesary — **necessary** *(circled)*
7. **peddler** *(circled)* — pedler — **pedlar** *(circled)*
8. **minuscule** *(circled)* — miniscule — minniscule
9. adress — adres — **address** *(circled)*
10. accomodate — **accommodate** *(circled)* — acommodate
11. iresistible — irresistable — **irresistible** *(circled)*
12. **liaison** *(circled)* — liaision — liason
13. harras — harrass — **harass** *(circled)*
14. **definitely** *(circled)* — definately — difinately
15. ocurence — **occurrence** *(circled)* — occurence
16. embarass — embaras — **embarrass** *(circled)*
17. pronounciation — pronounceation — **pronunciation** *(circled)*
18. independant — **independent** *(circled)* — indipendent
19. **questionnaire** *(circled)* — questionairre — questionaire
20. wiered *(struck/marked)* — **weird** *(circled)* — wierd
21. brocolli — broccolli — **broccoli** *(circled)*
22. refering — **referring** *(circled)* — refferring
23. **recommend** *(circled)* — recomend — reccommend
24. **cemetery** *(circled)* — semetary — cemetary

AMERICAN OR BRITISH STYLE OF SPELLING?

(p. 16)

	American	British	Both
1. honour	☐	☑	☐
2. meter	☐	☐	☑
3. mediaeval	☐	☐	☑
4. catalyze	☑	☐	☐
5. labor	☑	☐	☐
6. waggon	☐	☑	☐
7. favour	☐	☑	☐
8. neighbor	☑	☐	☐
9. travelling	☐	☑	☐
10. encyclopedia	☐	☐	☑
11. moustache	☐	☑	☐
12. color	☑	☐	☐
13. paralyse	☐	☑	☐
14. extol	☐	☐	☑
15. center	☑	☐	☐
16. dialogue	☐	☑	☐
17. molt	☑	☐	☐
18. analyse	☐	☑	☐
19. plow	☑	☐	☐
20. sulphur	☐	☑	☐
21. vigour	☐	☑	☐
22. skeptic	☑	☐	☐
23. catalog	☑	☐	☐
24. enrol	☐	☑	☐
25. archaeologist	☐	☐	☑
26. fulfil	☐	☑	☐
27. glamour	☐	☐	☑
28. theatre	☐	☑	☐
29. saviour	☐	☑	☐
30. distill	☑	☐	☐
31. litre	☐	☑	☐

OLD ENGLISH SPELLING

(p. 24)

Note: The fact that the word still exists with an altered spelling does *not* mean it necessarily has the same meaning today.

1.	æsc: ash	25.	niht: night
2.	bedd: bed	26.	ofen: oven
3.	cīese: cheese	27.	riht: right
4.	cild: child	28.	sǣ: sea
5.	circe: church	29.	sceaft: shaft
6.	clǣne: clean	30.	scēap: sheep
7.	cwēn: queen	31.	scield: shield
8.	dēofol: devil	32.	scilling: shilling
9.	ecg: edge	33.	scip: ship
10.	fisc: fish	34.	seofon: seven
11.	flǣsc: flesh	35.	siextig: sixty
12.	folc: folk	36.	stenc: stench
13.	gēar: year	37.	tōþ: tooth
14.	hecge: hedge	38.	þe: the
15.	heofone: heaven	39.	þicce: thick
16.	hlāford: lord	40.	þing: thing
17.	hors: horse	41.	þrī: three
18.	hring: ring	42.	þurh: through
19.	hwæl: whale	43.	tunge: tongue
20.	hwȳ: why	44.	wæter: water
21.	lēoht: light	45.	weg: way
22.	miht: might	46.	weorþ: worth
23.	mōnaþ: month	47.	woruld: world
24.	nacod: naked	48.	wrītan: write

THE E-CANCELLATION TEST

(p. 41)

A At th& b&ginning of th& tw&nti&th c&ntury, th&r& was a
larg& farm n&ar Los Ang&l&s call&d th& Hollywood Ranch.
A f&w d&cad&s lat&r, it was on& of th& most famous plac&s
in th& world. Th& first movi&s w&r& mad& in N&w York on
th& &ast Coast. But, as th&y us&d th& light of th& sun, th&
advantag&s of Los Ang&l&s soon b&cam& appar&nt, wh&r&
th&r& w&r& at l&ast thr&& hundr&d and fifty days of sun
&v&ry y&ar as w&ll as pictur&squ& natural sc&n&ry such as
mountains, b&ach&s and d&s&rt. Aft&r its h&yday in the
nin&t&&n thirti&s and nin&t&&n-forti&s, Hollywood had to
turn to t&l&vision films b&for& g&tting back to th& block-
bust&rs that dominat& movi& hous&s today. How&v&r its
position as th& plac& that produc&s most films has b&&n
ov&rtak&n by Bollywood in India. (93 "e"s.)

B Grac& Pain& liv&d in an isolat&d cottag& for most of h&r
lif&. In middl&-ag& sh& cam& to London, and was
astonish&d at city lif&. B&st of all sh& lov&d h&r cook&r
with its row of controls. On& day sh& told m& about h&r
amazing cook&r. Sh& had l&ft h&r whol& &v&ning m&al in
th& ov&n; at fiv& o'clock th& &l&ctric clock would switch it
on and by s&v&n a thr&& cours& m&al would b& r&ady to
w&lcom& h&r hom&. I almost &nvi&d h&r. But wh&n w&
n&xt m&t sh& r&lat&d what had actually occurr&d:
how&v&r automatic your cook&r, you hav& still got to
r&m&mb&r to turn it on. (66 "e"s.)

REASONS

Usually people fail to spot about five "e"s out of a hundred, i.e.
about seven in the two passages, mostly in the word "the." This
demonstrates that they pay attention to whole words rather than
just single letters. Some types of dyslexia are signaled by problems with "important" "e"s, such as the "e" in "den," which dis-
tinguishes it from "din" and "don" but not with "unimportant"
"e"s, such as the "e" in "waited," since there are no words spelled
"waitid" or "waitod."

ORTHOGRAPHIC
REGULARITIES TEST

(p. 56)

1. **blar**/blarh
2. ckole/**kole**
3. leck/ckel
4. **snove**/snov
5. tcheb/**cheb**
6. **chig**/tchig
7. blic/**blick**
8. fanq/**fanque**
9. **ster**/sterh
10. gneit/**teign**
11. nowh/**whon**
12. flij/**flidge**
13. huz/**huze**
14. **pluze**/pluz
15. staj/**stadge**
16. truv/**truve**
17. **whar**/rawh
18. gnope/**nope**
19. dgain/**jain**
20. **jarn**/narj
21. blav/**blave**
22. gnil/**lign**
23. **lutch**/tchul

24. **nait**/gnait/
25. **wras**/sawr
26. qish/**quish**
27. **quong**/qong
28. lerh/**rhell**
29. forh/**rhoff**
30. **smaze**/smaz
31. sniv/**snive**
32. frak/**frack**
33. spiwh/**spiw**
34. plawh/**plaw**
35. **terque**/terq
36. **squol**/squl
37. dgoll/**joll**
38. **klaze**/klaz
39. **nuft**/gnuft
40. gewr/**wreg**
41. **prew**/prewh
42. nartch/tcharn
43. **plock**/ploc
44. **blive**/bliv
45. **wrof**/fowr

Explanations
- "wh" occurs only at the beginning of words: when
- "ck" occurs only at the end: black
- "j" occurs at the beginning, "dge" at the end: judge
- "wr" occurs only at the beginning: write
- "ch" occurs at the beginning, "tch" at the end: chat, catch
- "v" occurs only at the end with a following "e": love
- single "z" occurs only at the end with an "e": laze
- "q" has to be followed by "u": quick

- "gn" has to occur at the end: sign
- "rh" has to occur at the beginning: rhubarb

Of course there are exceptions, such as "gneiss," "shiv," "catarrh," "Iraq" and "celeriac."

BRITISH VERSUS AMERICAN NEWSPAPERS

(p. 61)

1. American labor
2. American center
3. British moult
4. American dialog
5. American wagon
6. British neighbour
7. British moustache
8. American honor
9. American liter
10. British aluminium
11. American skeptic and catalog
12. British favour
13. American sulfur
14. British travelling

WORDS THAT ARE COMMONLY MISSPELLED

(p. 72)

1. choize — (choice) — choise
2. (sincerely) — sincerly — sincerelly
3. thier house is . . . — there house is . . . — (their) house is . . .
4. (really) — realy — reelly
5. develope — divelop — (develop)
6. (kindergarten) — kindegarten — kindergarden
7. becuse — becase — (because)
8. diffrint — (different) — diferent
9. govemment — goverment — (government)
10. busines affairs — busyness affairs — (business) affairs
11. (knowledge) — noledge — nollidge
12. profesional — (professional) — proffessional
13. wold — wou'd — (would)
14. I don't know (where) to go. — I don't know were to go. — I don't know wear to go.
15. superseed — supercede — (supersede)
16. (address) — adress — adresse
17. cariere — carier — (career)
18. (accommodation) — accomodation — acomodation
19. particuler — (particular) — partikular
20. intergrate — (integrate) — intigrate
21. (grammar) — grammer — gramar
22. descripe — (describe) — discribe
23. begining — (beginning) — biginning
24. (interesting) — intristing — intresting
25. the book wich . . . — the book (which) . . . — the book witch . . .

157

SOUNDS OR LETTERS?

(p. 80)

Answers and Explanation

Some words feel as if they had more sounds because of the extra letters. Many people judge "edge" to have more than 2 sounds (phonemes) because of its 4 letters. The same is true for "who" (2 sounds, 3 letters) and for "church" (3 sounds, 6 letters). In reverse, some words seem to have fewer sounds because they have fewer letters than sounds; "fix" seems to have fewer than 4, and "music" less than 6.

Here are the answers, giving the numbers of phonemes for each word.

1. bought	3	18. music	5	35. rich	3
2. box	4	19. judge	3	36. wing	3
3. thin	3	20. who	2	37. page	3
4. him	3	21. spend	5	38. unit	5
5. catch	3	22. age	2	39. me	2
6. the	2	23. it	2	40. cost	4
7. chop	3	24. think	4	41. she	2
8. crash	4	25. match	3	42. crop	4
9. of	2	26. chat	3	43. shock	3
10. edge	2	27. next	5	44. bat	3
11. fix	4	28. thought	3	45. let	3
12. do	2	29. land	4	46. trust	5
13. then	3	30. nothing	5	47. back	3
14. broccoli	7	31. ought	2	48. stamp	5
15. jet	3	32. win	3	49. past	4
16. light	3	33. stupid	6	50. washing	5
17. job	3	34. plant	5		

more sounds than letters: box, fix, next, unit (depending on accent "u" may be one or two sounds)

less sounds than letters: bought, thin, catch, the, chop, crash, edge, then, broccoli, light, judge, who, age, think, match, chat, thought, nothing, ought, rich, wing, page, she, shock, back, washing

same number of sounds and letters: him, of, jet, job, spend, it, land, win, plant, me, cost, crop, bat, let, trust, stamp, music, stupid

GUESS THE FIRST LANGUAGES

(p. 98)

Greek: Gambridge (1), revoluzion (18), leccons (20)
German: reseption (2), telefon (15), tink (21)
Spanish: proffessional (3), mentionned (5), photoes (10)
Japanese: vocaburaries (4), secondaly (16), subejects (19)
Italian: addresse (6), particulery (13)
Arabic: rutine (7), defacult (17)
French: familly (8), monney (12), enthousiastic (14)
Chinese: calld (9), endiveduoly (11)

HISTORY TEST

(p. 105)

F 1400 John of Trevisa, *Marvels of Britain*
A 1592 Nash, Thomas, *Pierce Penilesse his supplication to the diuell.*
D 1651 Milton, John, *The life and reigne of King Charls*
C 1775 Washington, George, INSTRUCTIONS TO COLONEL BENEDICT ARNOLD
E 1880 James, Henry, *Washington Square*
B 1981 Chomsky, Noam (ed. C. Otero), *Radical Priorities*

(p. 111)

			spelling group
1.	questionnaire	questionaire	1
2.	That's definate.	That's definite.	6
3.	supersede	supercede	3
4.	highly responsible	highly responsable	6
5.	accommodation	accomodation	1
6.	a complementary drink	a complimentary drink	2
7.	He critisised the plan.	He criticised the plan.	3
8.	an independent report	an independant report	5
9.	She refered to Bush.	She referred to Bush.	1
10.	open-ended categories	open-ended catagories	5
11.	quiet right	quite right	2
12.	good sense	good sence	3
13.	He achieved greatness.	He acheived greatness.	4
14.	seperate rooms	separate rooms	5
15.	liberal tendancy	liberal tendency	5
16.	ecstasy	ecstacy	3
17.	beginers' luck	beginner's luck	1
18.	sensative	sensitive	6
19.	They beleived the news.	They believed the news.	1
20.	the bare necessities	the bear necessities	2
21.	the percieved cost	the perceived cost	4
22.	the principal of gravity	the principle of gravity	2
23	not necessarily true	not necessarily true	1
24.	This is indispensable.	This is indispensible.	6
25.	It's their problem.	It's they're problem.	2
26.	an immence cliff	an immense cliff	3
27.	to conceive	to concieve	4
28	cause and affect	cause and effect	5
29.	He recieved a postcard.	He received a postcard.	4
30.	reversible	reversable	3

Explanations for What's Wrong with Your Spelling Test
This test indicates whether people have problems with particular areas of English spelling. To find the type of mistake involved, circle the spelling group number in the right-hand column for each word spelled incorrectly and then see which group has the most mistakes.

1. *Letter doubling (words 1, 5, 9, 17, 23):* one reason for doubling consonants is to show that the preceding vowel is "short"— "din" versus "dinner." See page 96.
2. *Homophones (words 6, 11, 20, 22, 25):* words that have the same pronunciation, or nearly so, but different spelling, such as "whole" versus "hole." See page 40.
3. *"c" or "s" (words 3, 7, 12, 16, 26):* rules about whether to write "s" or "c" for an "s" sound. Usually "c" is said as "s" before "e/i/y." "Supersede" is difficult because English spelling kept the distinction between two Latin words "cedere" (to go) "intercede" and "sedere" (to sit) "supersede." There are variations between English and American styles for words like "defense/defence." See page 76.
4. *"ie" or "ei" mistakes (words 13, 19, 21, 27, 29):* "i" before "e" except after "c" when the vowel sound is "ee." See page 46.
5. *"e" or "a" (words 8, 10, 14, 15, 28):* the correspondences for these letters vary in unstressed syllables. The "-ant/-ent" spellings are said in the same way. Some words follow the French "-ant" ending, "descendant," some the Latin "-ent," "independent." Often both are possible, "dependant/ dependent."
6. *"i/a" (words 2, 4, 18, 24, 30):* the correspondences for these letters are hard to predict in unstressed syllables. The difference between "-ible" and "-able" is tenuous. Some words, often ending in "s" sounds, follow the Latin "-ible"— "responsible." Others, tending to end in "d" or "t" sounds, follow the French "-able"—"dependable."

IDENTIFY THE LANGUAGE

(p. 125)

Note: these are the languages, not the plants' places of origin.

1. broccoli **Italian**
2. mangetout **French**
3. bok choi **Chinese**
4. okra **West African (Fante)**
5. zucchini **Italian**
6. lollo rosso **Italian**
7. avocado **Spanish**
8. chili **Spanish**
9. shiitake mushrooms **Japanese**
10. guava **Spanish**
11. primavera salad **Spanish**
12. coleslaw **Dutch**
13. papaya **Spanish**
14. mangosteen **Bahasa Malaysia**
15. kumquats **Chinese**
16. kiwifruit **Maori**
17. medjol dates **Arabic**
18. fuji apples **Japanese**
19. pistachios **Italian**
20. satsumas **Japanese**

TOLKIEN'S NAMES

(p. 133)

1. Balin **Dwarf**
2. Galadriel **Elf**
3. Eowen **Human**
4. Gimli **Dwarf**
5. Aragorn **Human**
6. Gandalf **Maiar**
7. Arwen **Elf**
8. Bombur **Dwarf**
9. Saruman **Maiar**
10. Bilbo **Hobbit**
11. Celeborn **Elf**
12. Meriadioc **Hobbit**
13. Fangorn **Other (Ent)**
14. Legolas **Elf**
15. Telchar **Dwarf**
16. Beren **Human**
17. Frodo **Hobbit**
18. Sauron **Maiar**
19. Theoden **Human**
20. Glorfindel **Elf**
21. Beleg **Elf**

ODD WORD OUT

(p. 135)

1.	**ch**	chicken	cheese	(chef)
2.	**ei**	(weigh)	ceiling	receive
3.	**x**	Xena	(X-ray)	xylophone
4.	**gh**	though	ought	(gherkin)
5.	**ow**	cow	(show)	now
6.	**c**	(cent)	call	Cuthbert
7.	**s**	ask	(bids)	scan
8.	**l**	(bill)	almond	almoner
9.	**e**	(ego)	egg	bed
10.	**m**	(mnemonic)	autumn	lemming
11.	**th**	this	then	(thin)
12.	**oa**	(abroad)	goat	load
13.	**a**	father	(chalk)	Brahms
14.	**oo**	food	(book)	brood
15.	**ph**	physics	Ralph	(shepherd)
16.	**y**	(city)	youth	you
17.	**au**	(sausage)	bauble	saucer
18.	**wh**	(whole)	whale	while
19.	**o**	above	(aroma)	cover
20.	**p**	(corps)	corpse	copse
21.	**u**	bun	but	(brute)
22.	**ae**	aeon	(aerial)	anaemia
23.	**h**	(house)	honest	hour
24.	**cc**	accept	succeed	(broccoli)
25.	**gu**	(tongue)	disguise	guard

AMERICAN VERSUS ENGLISH SPELLING AROUND THE WORLD

(p. 138)

British-style spelling: 1. fulfil, 4. dialogue, 7. travelling, 8. aluminium

American-style spelling: 2. favor, 3. jewelry, 5. plow, 6. archeologist

BRITISH AND AMERICAN NOVEL SPELLINGS

(p. 141)

American pop groups: 6 Teens, Eminem, Puddle of Mudd, Outlawz

American show dogs: Knot-A-Yacht, For-U-To-N-V, Mistymoor, Up N'Adam

American license plates: 2FAST4U, CHZHED, CYCOPTH, 8ɪTCH

American racehorses: Funny Cide, Iwontell, Hez Not Yours, Outatime

American hairdressers: Mane Street, Oassis Salon, Hair Dooz

American song titles: Emale, Bagg Up

ACKNOWLEDGMENTS

*   *   *

Major sources in putting together this book were the frequency list from the Brown University Corpus plus specific sources mentioned on individual pages, and indeed the streets of the places I have visited in the past five years in the United States, Canada, Ireland and elsewhere. The Web was an important resource, allowing one to discover hairdressers in Houston one minute, the number of wrong spellings for *receive* out of 37 million examples the next, the spellings of the original Shakespeare First Folio the next. Robert Cook searched out much of the information and coordinated its presentation. Some of the information and photos for this edition were kindly provided by Maria del Carmen De Avila; Nicky Cook; Iggy Roca; Cathy Walter and Dave, Robyn and Julie Newton.

Some of the same topics are treated in a more academic way in V. J. Cook (2004), *The English Writing System*, Arnold, and on the Web site *Writing Systems*, http://homepage.ntlworld.com/vivian.c/.

I am grateful to the Society of Authors, on behalf of the Bernard Shaw estate, for giving permission to quote from Bernard Shaw's preface to R. A. Wilson's *The Miraculous Birth of Language* (1941).

SOURCES OF INFORMATION

* * *

Brooks, G., Gorman, T., and Kendall, L. (1993) *Spelling It Out: The Spelling Abilities of 11- and 15-year-olds.* Slough, UK: National Foundation for Educational Research.

Carney, E. (1994) *A Survey of English Spelling.* London: Routledge.

Cook, V. J. (2004) *The English Writing System.* London: Edward Arnold.

Crain, P. (2000) *The Story of A.* Stanford University Press.

Diringer, D. (1962) *Writing.* London: Thames and Hudson.

Kucera, H., and Francis, W. N. (1967) *Computational Analysis of Present-day American English.* Providence: Brown University Press.

McIntosh, R. (1990) *Hyphenation.* Halifax: Hyphen House.

Oxford English Dictionary (OED) (1994) CD-ROM version 1.13, Oxford University Press.

Pound. L. (1926) "The Kraze for K." *American Speech* 1, 1, 43–44.

Roca, I., and Johnson, W. (1999) *A Course in Phonology.* Oxford: Blackwell.

Schwartz, A. (1974) *A Twister of Twists a Tangler of Tongues: Tongue Twisters.* London: Deutsch.

Seidenberg, M. S., and McClelland, J. L. (1989) "A Distributed, Developmental Model of Word Recognition and Naming." *Psychological Review* 96, 523–68.

Treiman, R. (1993) *Beginning to Spell: A Study of First-Grade Children.* Oxford: Oxford University Press.

Venezky, R. (1999) *The American Way of Spelling.* The Hague: Mouton.

THEME INDEX

* * *

To help readers to follow particular threads, the following list organizes the pages into themes.

Printed in the United States
By Bookmasters